The Effect of Education on Efficiency in Consumption

ROBERT T. MICHAEL
University of California, Los Angeles

OCCASIONAL PAPER 116

NATIONAL BUREAU OF
ECONOMIC RESEARCH
New York 1972

Distributed by Columbia University Press
New York and London

Contents

Tables,
Charts,
Figures

Acknowledgments

THIS PAPER is based on my doctoral dissertation submitted to Columbia University in 1969. The research was conducted at the National Bureau as part of the economics of education project funded by the Carnegie Corporation of New York, for whose financial assistance I am very grateful.

My principal indebtedness is to my thesis supervisor, Gary S. Becker. The theoretical chapters rest heavily upon his pioneering contributions to the theory of human capital and the concept of household production functions. In addition, I greatly appreciate the unselfish investment of his time in this project through constructive comments on all aspects of my work and at all stages of its development. The excellent training he offers students in the principles and techniques of economic research is in large measure responsible for my interest in applied economics.

Many individuals at the National Bureau have been very helpful to me. I particularly wish to express my appreciation to Jacob Mincer for several useful substantive suggestions regarding the theoretical framework developed here and its empirical implementation. Other members of the National Bureau's staff reading committee were V. K. Chetty and Finis Welch, both of whom made constructive comments on preliminary drafts of this paper. The members of the Board of Directors' reading committee, Robert A. Charpie, Robert M. Solow, and Henri Theil, also made useful comments for which I am most grateful. Michael Grossman made detailed comments on much of this work, and these as well as the many hours we spent discussing numerous points are much appreciated. I have also benefited from comments by Barry R. Chiswick, Isaac Ehrlich, Victor R. Fuchs, Gilbert R. Ghez, Yoel Haitovsky, F. Thomas Juster, Jacob Paroush, Sherwin Rosen, and members of the Labor Workshop at Columbia University.

I am grateful to Pamela Martens and Susan Sumner for their research assistance and to Sydney Jacobs and Martha Jones for their help in communicating with the computer. I appreciate the work of Hedy D. Jellinek, who carefully edited the manuscript. For research assistance, proofreading, and general encouragement I thank my wife, Nancy.

ROBERT T. MICHAEL

The Effect of Education
on Efficiency in Consumption

Introduction

WITHIN THE PAST decade human capital has become a popular focus of study by economists. Its relevance for dealing with issues of economic growth, aggregate productivity, wage structure, and distribution of personal income is now unquestioned. Since human capital is viewed as an investment good, much attention has been turned to the returns accruing on that investment. Most of the research along these lines has dealt with the effect of the investment on an individual's market earnings.

While the increase in market earnings is surely one aspect of the returns on human capital (investment in formal schooling, on-the-job training, good health, information about markets, and so forth), there is no reason to suppose it is the only return on that investment. A distinguishing characteristic of human capital is that it is embedded in an individual and therefore accompanies him wherever he goes—into the labor market, into the theater, into the voting booth, and into the kitchen. If, therefore, human capital affects productivity and yields a stream of income in one of these—the labor market—it seems reasonable to expect it to have some effect on productivity in other activities as well. As T. W. Schultz once suggested, the general proposition on which the interest in human capital rests is that "people enhance their capabilities as producers and as consumers by investing in themselves."[1] Yet in the literature very little attention has been paid to the effects of human capital on one's capabilities as a consumer or to its effects on productivity in activities outside the labor market. This study may be viewed as one of the attempts under way to fill this gap and to analyze and measure these nonmarket effects.

Clearly, the explanation for the imbalance in the study of nonmarket effects of human capital lies in the fact that no conceptual framework has been developed in which they may be analyzed. Fortunately, recent literature has suggested a new approach to consumption theory, which

[1] Theodore W. Schultz, "Reflections on Investment in Man," *Journal of Political Economy,* October 1962, supplement, p. 1.

3

can be used as a vehicle to study the nonmarket effects of human capital.[2] The theoretical model developed in this connection also appears to be useful in understanding some effects on behavior of numerous other factors, such as climate, political stability, population density, and so on.

The traditional theory of consumer behavior treats purchased goods as items directly entering the utility function of the consumer. When a good is purchased and consumed, the individual's utility is presumed to be enhanced. The new approach argues that the act of consumption is in fact a production activity, in which the consumer uses both market goods and his own time as inputs in the production of more basic desiderata called commodities. (For example, one uses a barber's services and some of one's own time to produce a groomed head of hair.) On the premise that purchased goods are not of direct utility to the consumer but are, rather, inputs used to produce commodities, the demand for market goods is a derived demand.[3]

Since this approach suggests that consumption involves a production process in the nonmarket sector, we may view human capital as affecting the efficiency of that process. Thus, the analytical tools of production theory may be applied to various aspects of consumption. An analytical framework in which these productivity effects of human capital may be viewed is outlined in the following chapters, which also develop certain implications for consumer behavior and report on empirical investigations of these implications.[4]

[2] See Gary S. Becker, "A Theory of the Allocation of Time," *Economic Journal,* September 1965; Kelvin Lancaster, "A New Approach to Consumer Demand," *Journal of Political Economy,* April 1966, and "Change and Innovation in the Technology of Consumption," *American Economic Review,* May 1966; and Richard Muth, "Household Production and Consumer Demand Functions," *Econometrica,* July 1966. This study most closely follows Becker's formulation.

[3] For some items this approach has long been in vogue. Keynes's discussion of the demand for money in terms of precautionary, speculative, and transaction demand can be interpreted as involving three commodities that use cash balances in their production; the demand for insurance clearly results from the desire for some form of security that can be produced using the purchased insurance policy as an input. It is only a small step from there to suggest that the demand for lawn mowers is essentially a demand for a factor of production used to produce an attractive lawn, that the demand for a doctor's services is a derived demand used in producing good health, or that the demand for food is a derived demand used in producing nutritional requirements.

[4] The theoretical model is one application of the household production function approach being explored at the National Bureau of Economic Research.

To summarize briefly: In the context of a set of household production functions, human capital is viewed as affecting the efficiency of the production process. By assuming Hicks-neutral productivity shifts, the effect of education on real income through nonmarket efficiency is examined, and it is suggested that changes in the level of education will lead to changes in the composition of the commodity basket. If education enhances nonmarket productivity, the consumption of commodities—and the expenditure on market goods—should shift toward luxuries. The empirical study investigates whether increases in education, *with money income fixed,* do in fact shift expenditure patterns in this manner.

The findings from several bodies of cross-sectional data reveal that the education level does affect expenditure patterns and generally does so in the expected manner, although in no sense perfectly coinciding with the predicted neutral shifts. Since the same items tend to be "nonneutral" in these various data and frequently tend to be so in the same direction, the effects of education appear to involve nonneutrality with respect to these items. From the coefficients estimated it is possible to infer something about the size of the contribution to real income from education's nonmarket effect. Thus, the elasticity of consumption income with respect to education is estimated to be around $+0.10$ by one estimating technique and as high as $+0.75$ by another. These estimates are admittedly rough and are suggested as no more than "ball park" estimates.

The theoretical framework of this study appears useful for explaining observed behavior, but other explanations can, of course, be put forth, and several of these are discussed throughout. The advantage of the model developed here is its capability to predict most of the observed shifts in expenditure patterns without the need for ad hoc theorizing. Futhermore, it does so with no complicating assumptions beyond the general presumptions of technological neutrality and linear homogeneity. As to those expenditure shifts that are not as predicted, the model can be used to interpret them in terms of ordinary price

See, for example, Gary S. Becker, "The Allocation of Time and Goods Over Time," NBER, June 1967, mimeo.; Gary S. Becker and Robert T. Michael, "On the Theory of Consumer Demand," March 1970, mimeo.; Gilbert R. Ghez, "A Theory of Life Cycle Consumption," Ph.D. dissertation, Columbia University, 1970; and Michael Grossman, "The Demand for Health: A Theoretical and Empirical Investigation," NBER, forthcoming.

effects (although empirically these effects cannot, as yet, be dealt with). While the conclusion is tentative, the empirical work suggests that this model is a viable one and that it offers a reasonably consistent interpretation of the effects of education on consumer behavior. Given the exploratory nature of the study, the results are encouraging and suggest that this new approach to the nonmarket sector merits further consideration in future research.

1

Human Capital and Consumption: The Theoretical Framework

THIS CHAPTER PRESENTS a conceptual framework in which the effects of human capital on nonmarket or consumption efficiency can be analyzed. The model is developed in the context of a general human capital variable, H, with the household as the unit of analysis. The effect of H on the productivity of the various production functions, on the relative prices of commodities, and on real full income is discussed in the first part of the chapter. The second part suggests some implications regarding the demand for commodities, for factors of production, and, briefly, for H itself.

THE ROLE OF AN ENVIRONMENTAL VARIABLE

Suppose the household has some utility function

$$U = u(Z_1, Z_2, \cdots, Z_n), \tag{1.1}$$

where the Z's are various commodities produced by the household according to the production functions

$$Z_i = f_i(x_i, t_i; H). \tag{1.2}$$

The x_i is a vector of market goods, t_i is the household's own time input in the production of commodity i, and H represents the household's available quantity of some environmental variable. The household has some money income

$$Y_m = wt_w + V = \sum_{i=1}^{n} x_i p_{x_i}, \tag{1.3}$$

where w is its wage rate in the labor market, t_w is the time spent in the labor market, and V is its nonwage income for the period.[1] Given an appropriately inclusive definition of market goods, the money income is equal to the total money expenditure. The household also has some fixed amount of time at its disposal, t, which it uses in the production of the commodities and in the labor market:

$$t = \sum_{i=1}^{n} t_i + t_w .$$ (1.4)

Equations (1.3) and (1.4) can be combined into one full income constraint on the household's utility maximization:[2]

$$Y = wt + V = \sum_{i=1}^{n} (x_i p_{x_i} + wt_i).$$ (1.5)

In this framework the household is viewed as a small firm producing many products, called commodities, from which it derives utility. The environmental variable, H, affects production by influencing the conditions in which production takes place, the nature of the productive processes, or the effective quantities of the direct inputs of time and market goods. The environmental variable is distinguished from the direct inputs by the fact that production of a commodity uses up some of the household's available time and market goods but does not, in general, affect the quantity of the environmental variable.[3]

The variable H was defined as a human capital variable, but it may be interpreted more broadly to encompass any factor affecting the household's nonmarket productivity, excluding the direct factors of production themselves. Certain environmental variables—for example, the degree of political stability, the level of hygiene and sanitation, the rate of literacy, the climate—might affect all households in a particular geographical location in a similar manner, and their effects would be studied in interregional or international comparisons. On the other hand, the influence of variables like the family's size, its age structure, and its stock of some form of human capital (such as formal schooling

---

[1] While the wage earnings of each family member might be treated separately, for simplicity's sake this will not be done here.

[2] In order to make this chapter more readable, the mathematical proofs of most of the statements are relegated to an appendix. Consequently, Appendix A roughly parallels the development in this chapter, but includes very little verbal description of the material.

[3] While the opportunity cost of using the environmental variable in producing

or the level of health), which affect each household individually, would be observed in an interhousehold comparison. While the model is developed here with the latter comparison in mind, the general framework is clearly applicable to interregional differences as well.

To analyze the effect of H on the production of a given commodity, we differentiate the production function with respect to H, holding the levels of x_i and t_i constant, which yields the marginal product of H in the production of Z_i. Assuming the production function to be homogeneous of the first degree in the direct factors x_i and t_i,

$$\left.\frac{dZ_i}{dH}\right|_{x_i,\, t_i} = MP_i = \left(x_i \frac{\partial MP_{x_i}}{\partial H} + t_i \frac{\partial MP_{t_i}}{\partial H}\right), \qquad (1.6)$$

or, using the convention that a tilde indicates a percentage change per unit change in H,

$$\widetilde{MP}_i = W_{x_i}\widetilde{MP}_{x_i} + W_{t_i}\widetilde{MP}_{t_i}, \qquad (1.7)$$

where the weights are the production shares and the sum of the weights is unity. Equation (1.7) states that the environmental variable's marginal product in the production of Z_i is a weighted average of its effect on the productivity of the direct inputs. Since in general the effect on the marginal products of the factors may be positive or negative, so, too, may $\widetilde{MP}_i$; that is, the environmental variable may increase or decrease the productivity of the factors.

As a complement to (1.7), one might ask what effect H has on the price of the commodity Z_i. Defining Π_i as the average price of Z_i, the effect of H on Π_i, evaluated at a fixed level of Z_i, is simply

$$\widetilde{\Pi}_i = -\widetilde{MP}_i, \qquad (1.8)$$

which suggests, for example, that a 3 per cent increase in the productivity of a linear homogeneous production function lowers the price of the commodity by 3 per cent.

While the analysis is developed in terms of the commodity Z_i, the environmental variable H may affect the production of each Z in the household's commodity basket. If H has different effects on the various production functions, it will affect the relative prices of the commodities.

any commodity may be zero, this does not imply that changing the level of H is costless. Determining the optimal level of the environmental variable is discussed at the end of this chapter.

In the most general case, H may have a different effect on each factor's marginal product in each production function, and these may differ in sign as well as in magnitude. Even if all the absolute price changes have the same sign, relative prices may be affected.[4]

In order to analyze these relative price effects more explicitly, define a price level as

$$\Pi = \Pi_1{}^{s_1}, \Pi_2{}^{s_2}, \ldots, \Pi_n{}^{s_n}, \tag{1.9}$$

where s_i is the expenditure share on commodity i and the sum of the shares equals unity.[5] Then the aggregate effect of an increase in H can be expressed as

$$\widetilde{\Pi} = \sum_i s_i \widetilde{\Pi}_i = -\sum_i s_i \widetilde{MP}_i. \tag{1.10}$$

That is, the percentage change in the price level is a weighted average of the productivity effects of H on the various production functions, with the direction of the effect reversed. Since the relative price of Z_i is Π_i/Π, the change in the relative price resulting from an increase in H would be

$$\widetilde{\Pi_i/\Pi} = \widetilde{\Pi}_i - \widetilde{\Pi}. \tag{1.11}$$

There is an alternative method of evaluating the effect of the environmental variable that involves computing the value of the marginal

---

[4] This can be illustrated with a very simple case. Suppose that for all commodities $\widetilde{MP}_{t_i} = \widetilde{MP}_{t_j} \neq \widetilde{MP}_{x_i} = \widetilde{MP}_{x_j}$; that is, H has the same percentage effect on the productivity of time used in all activities and also a different but equal effect on the productivity of all goods used in all activities. Suppose, furthermore, that H affects the productivity of the time input more than the productivity of the goods input, i.e., $\widetilde{MP}_t > \widetilde{MP}_x$. In such a case the effect of H on the productivity of the function i or on the price of Z_i would be greater the more time-intensive the production of Z_i. Since $\widetilde{\Pi}_i$ is simply a weighted average of the inputs' productivity effects and the weights are production shares, under these assumed conditions the ranking of the $\widetilde{\Pi}_i$ would be exactly the same as the ranking of the time intensities if the substitution elasticities did not differ greatly. The *relative* prices of those commodities that were relatively time-intensive would fall (if the $\widetilde{MP}$ were positive) and the relative prices of commodities that were relatively goods-intensive would rise.

[5] A geometric or logarithmic mean is used since our interest is in averaging percentage changes in these prices. Although (1.9) is called a price level, it uses fixed weights, and a price index would simply be the ratio of Π in one period or one situation to $\Pi°$, the base period's price level.

product of H in each productive activity and summing these VMP_i. Intuitively, the sum of these dollar values is a measure of H's effect on real income. Let

$$VMP_i = \Pi_i(MP_i) = \Pi_i Z_i(\widetilde{MP}_i),$$

then, summing over all commodities,

$$\widetilde{Y}_c = \sum_i (VMP_i)/Y = \sum_i s_i(\widetilde{MP}_i). \tag{1.12}$$

$\widetilde{Y}_c$ will be called the "change in consumption income." VMP_i is the value of the additional units of Z_i resulting from a unit increase in H; the sum of the VMP_i is then the total value of H's effect. $\widetilde{Y}_c$ expresses this total value as a percentage of full income. The term abstracts completely from any effects of H on market earnings, but incorporates the nonmarket effects. From equations (1.10) and (1.12)

$$\widetilde{Y}_c = \sum_i s_i(\widetilde{MP}_i) = -\widetilde{\Pi}. \tag{1.13}$$

Thus, a change in H which affects nonmarket productivity may be evaluated as either a reduction in the cost of achieving a given output or as an increase in the output of commodities, holding the levels of the factors of production constant.

The household's full income, Y, defined by equation (1.5), combines price level, Π, reflects its capacity to convert these time and money re- its time and money resources into a single constraint. The household's sources into commodities. Reductions in market prices of goods or increases in the efficiency with which commodities are produced lower the household's price level. The household's "real full income" may be defined as (Y/Π), which indicates its resource constraint expressed in real terms. So, for example, if H adversely affects nonmarket productivity, households with higher levels of H will have a higher price level and a lower real full income. Since the probable direction of H's effect depends upon the nature of the environmental variable, no hypothesis has been formulated as yet. The model simply suggests a framework in which the influence of an environmental variable on the household's real income may be analyzed.

THE IMPLIED EFFECTS ON THE HOUSEHOLD'S DEMAND

Through its effect on the marginal products of the direct inputs, H can change the relative prices of the commodities and can alter the real income of the household. Thus, the usual analysis would suggest that H would create substitution and income effects on the demand for the commodities; that is, H would alter the optimal basket of commodities. If we write the demand function for commodity Z_i as

$$Z_i^d = d_i \left(\frac{Y}{\Pi}, \frac{\Pi_i}{\Pi} \right), \qquad (1.14)$$

where the arguments are real income and the relative price of Z_i, H's effect on Z_i^d, abstracting from its effects on money income, would be[6]

$$\widetilde{Z}_i^d = \eta_i(\widetilde{Y}_e) + \epsilon_i(\widetilde{\Pi}_i - \widetilde{\Pi}) \qquad (1.15)$$

where $\widetilde{Z}_i^d = (dZ_i^d/dH)/Z_i^d$ and η_i and ϵ_i are the commodity's income and own price elasticity. The first term in (1.15) is the income effect, which will be positive for any "normal" good if H's nonmarket effect on real income is positive; the second term is the substitution effect— if H is biased toward Z_i, $|\widetilde{\Pi}_i| > |\widetilde{\Pi}|$ and its relative price falls, and since $\epsilon_i < 0$, the effect on Z_i^d is positive. If the productivity effects on Z_i is equal to the average productivity effect, $\widetilde{\Pi}_i = \widetilde{\Pi}$ and the substitution term drops out.

Similarly, if an increase in H affects the optimal quantity of the commodities, it would be expected to affect the derived demand for the factors x_i and t_i. From production function (1.2), the percentage change in the demand for factor x_i per unit change in H would be

$$\widetilde{x}_i = (\widetilde{Z}_i^d - \widetilde{MP}_i) + w_{t_i}(\widetilde{x}_i - \widetilde{t}_i), \qquad (1.16)$$

where w_t is the production share. If the production function is homogeneous, and H is assumed not to affect the ratio of factor prices, p_x/p_t, then the evaluation of $(\widetilde{x}_i - \widetilde{t}_i)$ in equilibrium gives

$$\widetilde{x}_i = (\widetilde{Z}_i^d - \widetilde{MP}_i) + w_{t_i}\sigma(\widetilde{MP}_{x_i} - \widetilde{MP}_{t_i}), \qquad (1.17)$$

where σ is the elasticity of substitution in production $(\sigma \geq 0)$; substituting (1.15) and rearranging,

$$\widetilde{x}_i = \eta_i\widetilde{Y}_e - \widetilde{MP}_i + \epsilon_i(\widetilde{\Pi}_i - \widetilde{\Pi}) + w_{t_i}\sigma(\widetilde{MP}_{x_i} - \widetilde{MP}_{t_i}). \qquad (1.18)$$

The first term on the right indicates the gross increase in the demand

[6] See section 5 of Appendix A for the derivations of equations (1.15) through (1.18).

for Z_i resulting from the effect of H on real income; the second represents the change in the production of Z_i from the initial quantities of the inputs, and the third represents the influence of commodity bias. The sum of these three terms indicates the net change in Z_i demanded—a demand which is met by altering the quantities of the factors of production. The final term shows the effect of factor bias— if H enhances productivity and is biased toward x, $\widetilde{MP}_x > \widetilde{MP}_t > 0$, and the final term is positive.

The human capital variable H has been viewed as an exogenous variable throughout this chapter. The model indicates the effects of H on utility maximization without developing the implications for the optimal stock of H. To the extent productivity in nonmarket activities is altered by H, the return on an investment in H is also affected. Ceteris paribus, if consumption efficiency is enhanced by human capital, the return will be larger, and if the marginal return is increased, the household will be induced to increase its stock of H.

Clearly, the human capital variable could be incorporated in the analysis as an endogenous variable, with consumption income treated as a return on the investment in H. In this way the effect of human capital on consumption—on the activities associated with nonmarket time—would be included in the evaluation of H as an investment prospect. In addition to investigating the return through earnings in the market sector, one would also investigate the return through productivity in the nonmarket sector. The sum of these pecuniary and consumption effects is a more adequate reflection of the full return on the investment. It is these consumption income effects that are the focus of this study.

2

Education as an Environmental Variable

CHAPTER 1 INTRODUCED a general model dealing with the manner in which an environmental variable may affect nonmarket production. The analysis was presented in the context of a general human capital variable, and it was shown that such a variable, by altering the productivity of the factors of production and thereby affecting the relative efficiency of the production functions, could change the real income of the individual household and create income and substitution effects. Chapter 2 will further develop this framework by focusing on one particular form of human capital—education—and by examining implications of the analysis that are empirically testable.

The most direct approach to the question of efficiency in production is an investigation of the output per unit of input, but for our purposes this is not feasible. Since the output has not been quantified (or even identified) in the case of most of the commodities considered here, a more indirect approach had to be used. Rather than observing differences in output as efficiency changes, the analysis is developed in terms of changes in market goods inputs that result from productivity shifts. This chapter discusses the changes in expenditures on market goods that productivity shifts would be expected to produce.

EDUCATION AND THE NEUTRALITY ASSUMPTION

Of the environmental variables mentioned in the preceding chapter, the human capital variable is probably the one most directly controlled by the household. So, from the point of view of policy decisions within the household, information about the nonmarket return on formal schooling, health, and so forth should be the first order of business.[1] Since much of the empirical work on the effect of human capital on market earnings has dealt with formal schooling, it seems likely that in the area of nonmarket effects this form of human capital may similarly be most manageable. Furthermore, estimates of market returns on investments in formal schooling are readily available for comparison with returns through nonmarket activities. Accordingly, the specific variable considered in this chapter and in the subsequent empirical work is the level of formal education.[2]

Since the equations in Chapter 1 are expressed in terms of any environmental variable H, we may apply them directly to an analysis of the effects of formal education on nonmarket activities. Thus, define

$$\widetilde{MP}_i{}^E \equiv \frac{\partial Z_i}{\partial E}\Big|Z_i;\ \widetilde{MP}_{x_i}{}^E \equiv \frac{\partial MP_{x_i}}{\partial E}\Big|MP_{x_i};\ \text{etc.},$$

and the effects on relative prices, consumption income, and the demand for commodities and factors will be defined in a perfectly analogous manner. In the interest of making the model empirically viable, a few important assumptions are imposed on the system at this point. First, we shall assume that education has a neutral effect on the productivity of the factors of production. Education will be considered "factor neutral" if

$$\widetilde{MP}_{x_i}{}^E = \widetilde{MP}_{t_i}{}^E = \widetilde{MP}_i{}^E. \tag{2.1}$$

This is a Hicksian definition of neutrality. In equilibrium the ratio of a factor's marginal product to its price is equal for all factors. Then, if education raises the marginal product of each factor by the same percentage, there is no induced substitution in production. Since in the case of factor neutrality the percentage effect of education is the same on all inputs, it is also equal to the percentage effect on the productivity of the function.

Further, it will be assumed that education has a neutral effect on the

---

[1] From the point of view of society as a whole, the return on investments in increased literacy, better hygiene, and so forth is also relevant. But, since the stock of human capital in society is also affected by government policy, it is no less relevant at the macro level.

[2] To the extent that age is considered a proxy for on-the-job experience, this form of human capital is also investigated empirically.

productivity of all production functions. Education will be called "commodity neutral" if

$$\widetilde{MP}_i{}^E = \widetilde{MP}_j{}^E = \widetilde{MP}^E. \tag{2.2}$$

This definition is also Hicks-neutral. If the productivity of all production processes is changed by the same percentage there is no induced substitution in consumption. Commodity neutrality and equation (1.8) imply

$$\widetilde{\Pi}_i = \widetilde{\Pi}_j = \widetilde{\Pi}, \tag{2.3}$$

i.e., that there are no relative price effects. Equation (1.13) also collapses to

$$\widetilde{Y}_c = \widetilde{MP}_i{}^E = -\widetilde{\Pi} \qquad \text{(for all } i\text{)} \tag{2.4}$$

with the assumption of commodity neutrality. This is evident, for if education affects the efficiency of each production function by r per cent, the change in consumption income is also r per cent. Commodity neutrality does not require factor neutrality and vice versa. Only in the presence of both does an increase in education change the productivity of all factors in all production functions by precisely the same percentage.

Although these neutrality assumptions place substantial restrictions on the model and possibly tax its realism, they do not limit its usefulness as severely as it may seem. The neutrality model permits analysis of education's effect on real income and the consequent shifts in consumption patterns as income changes. Certain hypotheses can be tested empirically, and from one point of view we can infer from the empirical findings the extent to which the neutrality assumptions are inappropriate.[3]

The substance of the model as it stands does not tell us whether a particular environmental variable improves or diminishes nonmarket efficiency; it is, rather, a means by which we can analyze the results on prices, opportunities, and behavior of any given efficiency effect.

[3] The restrictions are imposed solely due to limitations in the availability of relevant data, and not to any inability of the model to deal with substitution effects. Dealing with productive activities conducted primarily in the home, we have few quantitative measures of the output and only scant information on the allocation of one of the two major inputs, time. As additional data become available—for example, household time budget studies—some of the assumptions of neutrality may be relaxed.

The working hypothesis pertaining to the direction of education's effect on nonmarket efficiency shall be

$$\widetilde{Y}_e > 0. \tag{2.5}$$

That is, education raises nonmarket productivity and thereby increases the household's real full income. The analytical framework developed in the previous chapter does not imply this hypothesis, but it is in the context of that framework that the hypothesis is formulated. If households engage in production in the nonmarket sector, education may affect the efficiency with which that production takes place.

There are at least two reasons for expecting the effect on efficiency to be positive. First, there is the well-documented positive correlation between levels of schooling and wages. From marginal productivity theory we infer a positive relationship between one's education and the productivity of his time in the labor market. Since education is embedded in the individual, if it affects the productivity of his time favor-.ably in productive activities in the labor market, it may be expected to do so in other productive activities as well. If education raises the productivity of one's time in nonmarket production, it thereby lowers the costs or increases the efficiency of nonmarket production, other things held constant.

Second, the level of education may affect productivity in the household for the same reasons that the level of technology affects productivity in the firm. For the latter, technology represents the acquisition and adoption of new knowledge or new productive techniques; for the former, education represents exposure to knowledge and perhaps the development of a receptive attitude toward the use of new information. The household chooses its productive techniques and selects the market goods and services with which it combines its own time to produce commodities, so the level of its managerial skill and the proficiency with which it purchases and uses market goods influence the level of efficiency in its nonmarket production. These skills will be favorably affected by education if the more educated individual possesses more knowledge (including more knowledge of how to acquire, evaluate, and utilize additional relevant information) and is more receptive to new ideas, including improved consumer products.[4] Since the house-

---

[4] For an excellent discussion of a related point dealing with the way in which education might influence productivity through a "worker effect" and an "allocative effect," see Finis Welch, "Education in Production," *Journal of Political Economy,* January 1970.

hold members both organize and engage in nonmarket production, the effects of education on the productivity of their own time input and on the efficiency with which production is organized are expected to lower the absolute cost of production or raise the real income of the household.

Thus, the hypothesis will be that education increases productivity in the household. This leads to certain predictions about the effect of education on consumption patterns. If the observed effect of education on expenditure patterns were precisely the opposite of the one suggested by the hypothesis, this would be consistent with education having an adverse effect on nonmarket productivity.[5] Again, the analytical framework developed here is not wedded to the hypothesis that the change in consumption income is positive. It would involve no substantive difference in the empirical analysis if the direction of education's effect were reformulated as an open question.

With the assumptions of factor and commodity neutrality, all relative price effects are eliminated both in production and in consumption. Thus, the nonmarket effect on the demand for the commodity Z_i is given by the simplified equation (1.15):

$$\widetilde{Z}_i{}^d = \eta_i(\widetilde{Y}_c), \qquad (2.6)$$

where the tilde now represents the percentage change per unit of education. The effect of education on the demand for the commodity will be positive if Z_i is "superior," under the hypothesis that $\widetilde{Y}_c > 0$.[6] The effect of education on the demand for Z_i will be greater the larger its consumption income effect and the larger the income elasticity.

Similarly, the equation for the derived demand for a factor of production (1.18) can be simplified given the assumption of factor neutrality. Since $\widetilde{MP}_{x_i} = \widetilde{MP}_{t_i}$, we get [7]

---

[5] The results can also imply that education has *no* nonmarket effect on efficiency ($\widetilde{Y}_c = 0$). This would be the case, for example, if education had no effect on expenditure patterns.

[6] A commodity is "superior" if its income elasticity, η, is positive; "inferior," if $\eta < 0$; a "luxury," if $\eta > 1$; and a "necessity," if $\eta < 1$. The terms are used according to these standard definitions and no value judgment or normative connotation is implied.

[7] Since $\widetilde{Y}_c = -\widetilde{\Pi}$ and $\widetilde{\Pi}_i = -\widetilde{MP}_i$, equation (2.7) can also be expressed as

$$\widetilde{x}_i = \widetilde{Y}_c(\eta_i - 1) + (\widetilde{\Pi}_i - \widetilde{\Pi})(\epsilon_i + 1),$$

which indicates that if the price elasticity of the commodity is unity, there is

$$\tilde{x}_i = \eta_i \tilde{Y}_c - \widetilde{MP}_i + \epsilon_i(\tilde{\Pi}_i - \tilde{\Pi}), \qquad (2.7)$$

or, from (1.15),

$$\tilde{x}_i = \tilde{Z}_i{}^d - \widetilde{MP}_i{}^E. \qquad (2.8)$$

Equation (2.8) suggests, for example, that if the percentage effect on the demand for Z_i were 6 per cent and the productivity effect for Z_i were 4 per cent, the change in education would induce a 2 per cent change in the quantity of x_i and t_i demanded.

Combining (2.6) and (2.8), and noting that under the commodity neutrality assumption $\widetilde{MP}_i{}^E = \tilde{Y}_c$,

$$\tilde{x}_i = \tilde{Y}_c(\eta_i - 1). \qquad (2.9)$$

Thus, the prediction of the neutrality model would be that

$$\tilde{x}_i \gtrless 0 \qquad \text{as} \qquad \eta_i \gtrless 1. \qquad (2.10)$$

If the commodity Z_i is a necessity, $\tilde{x}_i < 0$, i.e., the consumer will reduce his expenditure on x_i; if the commodity Z_j is a luxury, $\tilde{x}_j > 0$, that is, the expenditure on x_j rises and is "financed" partly from the reduced expenditure on x_i. Since the consumer's money income is held fixed in this discussion, his total expenditure is fixed.[8]

Education's effect on the demand for commodities and market goods is interpreted here in terms of changes in relative prices and in real income through a reduction in the price level. An alternative way of expressing the same model is to suggest that by increasing the output of the various commodities, education raises total utility (by the sum of the additional amounts of each Z_i expressed in utility-equivalent

---

no induced effect on the demand for the factor, even if the relative prices of the commodities are affected.

[8] Multiplying each derived demand equation (2.9) of the household by its expenditure share and summing over all goods:

$$s_i\tilde{x}_i = s_i(\tilde{Y}_c\eta_i - \tilde{Y}_c)$$

$$\sum_i s_i\tilde{x}_i = \tilde{Y}_c \left(\sum_i s_i\eta_i\right) - \tilde{Y}_c \sum_i s_i$$

$$= \tilde{Y}_c - \tilde{Y}_c$$

$$= 0.$$

units) and thereby shifts the relative demand for Z's toward those with higher utility elasticities.[9]

While the latter interpretation views the model in utility terms, it is not an alternative model in any essential way but simply a translation into another language. An alternative can be developed, however, that can lead to the same predicted behavior pattern and is couched in terms of a change in tastes. Suppose that education, for whatever reason, directly increased one's total satisfaction or utility, not through any productivity effects but by simply altering the utility function (i.e., by changing tastes). In this case, education indirectly alters the relative marginal utilities of the Z's in a specific manner if the utility function is not homogeneous.[10]

Since relative prices of commodities are not affected in this "tastes" interpretation, in equilibrium the ratio of the marginal utilities would be the same as initially. Consequently, by diminishing the marginal rate of substitution in consumption, education induces shifts toward items with higher utility elasticities and away from those with lower elasticities—the same qualitative effects as the productivity model implies. Notice, though, that in order to get the same predicted response in behavior, the presumed effect of education on the utility function involves a fundamental and specific change in the indifference map.[11]

EMPIRICAL IMPLICATIONS OF NEUTRALITY

Equation (2.9) suggests the empirical test of the model. If real income is augmented by the efficiency effect of education, the term $\tilde{Y}_e$ will be positive. Accordingly, if the income elasticity of a commodity is greater than unity, the equation implies that the expenditure on the market goods associated with that commodity will be positively related to education. Then holding the household's money income constant

[9] For a more detailed exposition of this point, see Appendix A, section 6.

[10] If all utility elasticities or income elasticities were equal, the neutral productivity model would predict no effect on behavior; the corresponding assumption here is homogeneity of the utility function, which would imply no effect on the ratios of marginal utilities. It is the *lack* of homogeneity that leads to the implication of an effect on behavior in both the neutral productivity model and the "tastes" model.

[11] For a more thorough discussion of this point, see the exposition and diagram in Appendix A, section 7.

and raising its level of education will lead to increased expenditure on market goods associated with luxuries and to decreased expenditure on goods associated with necessities.

The economic interpretation suggested by the model for this predicted behavior pattern is the following. Education increases efficiency in all activities in the nonmarket sector and is assumed to have the same effect on each activity. Thus, relative prices of commodities are unchanged, but the price index falls or real income rises, with money income held fixed. The rise in real income induces the household to increase its demand for commodities, the amount of the increase being shown by the income effect $(\eta_i \tilde{Y}_c)$. At the same time the household is "supplied" with $\widetilde{MP}_i$ additional amount of each commodity. The effect on the demand for the market input clearly depends on whether the increased demand for commodity i, $(\eta_i \tilde{Y}_c)$, or the increased supply of commodity i, $\widetilde{MP}_i$, is greater. If the household is supplied with more of the commodity than it demands (this is the case when $\eta_i < 1$) it will *reduce* its inputs to bring its total production into line with its demand, and conversely, if its demand exceeds its total production it will increase its use of market inputs. It is, then, an implication of the neutrality model that as education rises, with money income held fixed, we expect to observe shifts in consumption patterns *as if* money income were increasing. Since we cannot directly observe the shifts in the consumption of commodities, we observe the resulting shifts in market goods instead.

Finally, from equation (2.9) it is possible to infer the magnitude of the change in consumption income $\tilde{Y}_c$. Multiplying through by the level of education converts the terms in equation (2.9) into elasticities: ϵ_{iE}, the elasticity of expenditure on the market good with respect to education; ϵ_{Y_cE} is the elasticity of consumption income with respect to education. Thus, from observations on the income elasticity, η_i, and the elasticity of expenditure on the market good with respect to education, ϵ_{iE}, the elasticity of consumption income can be computed:

$$\epsilon_{Y_cE} = \epsilon_{iE}/(\eta_i - 1). \qquad (2.11)$$

This elasticity, ϵ_{Y_cE}, abstracts from changes in money income and indicates the effect of education on real full income through changes in nonmarket productivity.

3

The Engel Curve

THE PRECEDING ANALYSIS suggests that as a household's education level rises the composition of its consumption basket will shift in the same manner as it does when money income rises. To determine whether this predicted response is in fact observed, we must identify the nature of shifts in consumption that accompany a rising income and ascertain whether they also occur with a rising level of education, holding money income stationary. This is done by estimating income-expenditure curves (Engel curves) from cross-sectional data and observing the separate, partial effects of income and education on the expenditure patterns of households. The forms and variables used in the estimating equation are discussed in the following pages.

THE FORM OF THE FUNCTION

The Engel curve fitted to the cross-sectional data is of the general form

$$X_i = f_i(Y, E, F, A, R) \tag{3.1}$$

where X_i is the household's expenditure on the market good i, Y is the measure of the household's income level, E is its level of education, and $F, A,$ and R are family size, age, and geographical region, respectively. (The rationale for including each variable as well as a discussion of the specific variable used in each case are the subject of the latter part of this chapter.) By the usual multiple regression techniques estimates are obtained of the partial effects of these variables on the expenditure X_i. Of principal interest from the point of view of the model is the relationship between the income and education coefficients.

The relationship (3.1) between the expenditure on the market good and the level of income and several other variables is, as in all such studies, only a partial relationship. The actual level of the expenditures is influenced by factors not directly quantifiable by the economist. What is implied by the Engel curve analysis is not that income, education, and other specified factors fully determine the expenditure pattern, but, rather, that changes in the level of income, et cetera, are closely associated with changes in expenditures on goods. The other factors that determine the level of expenditures are presumed to be unrelated in any systematic way to the explanatory variables included here. Thus, systematic differences in expenditures between households are presumed to be related to these economic variables.

It should be noted that, while the analysis applies to the income elasticity of the commodity, η_i, the elasticity obtained from fitting (3.1) is η_{xi}, the income elasticity of expenditure on the market good. If the market good x_i is used in the production of several commodities, it can be shown that, if each unit of x_i is used exclusively in the production of one Z, then

$$\eta_{x_i} = \sum_h k_h \eta_{z_h}, \tag{3.2}$$

i.e., the income elasticity of the market good is equal to a weighted average of the income elasticities of the commodities which use that good, where the weights are the share of the good expended on each commodity.[1] If a unit of x_i is used jointly in the production of two or more commodities, relative prices of commodities are affected by the level of production of other commodities, and the distinction between environmental variables and direct inputs breaks down.[2] This issue will not be pursued here.

It should also be noted that the estimated income elasticities are gross elasticities. The effect of changes in the value of time accompanying

---

[1] Say x_i is used in the production of m commodities Z_h $(h = 1, 2, \ldots, m)$, so that x_{i1} is used in producing Z_1, x_{i2}, in producing Z_2, etc., and $\sum_h x_{ih} = x_i$, then, with a constant price of x_i,

$$\eta_{xi} = \frac{dX_i}{dY}\frac{Y}{X_i} = \sum_h \frac{dX_{ih}}{dY}\frac{Y}{X_i} = \sum_h \eta_{zh}\left(\frac{dX_{ih}}{dZ_h}\frac{Z_h}{X_{ih}}\right)\frac{X_{ih}}{X_i},$$

but with linear homogeneous production functions and factors changing proportionately,

$$\left(\frac{dX_{ih}}{dZ_h}\frac{Z_h}{X_{ih}}\right) = 1$$

or

$$\eta_{xi} = \sum_h \eta_{zh}k_h,$$

where k_h is the share of x_i used in the production of Z_h.

[2] For one application of this joint production problem, see Michael Grossman, "The Demand for Health: A Theoretical and Empirical Investigation," NBER, forthcoming.

changes in income will be reflected in these income elasticities. By the assumptions discussed in Chapter 2, however, the nonmarket education effect on real income is assumed to be a pure income effect, hence ideally the income elasticities would be estimated with the value of time held constant. An increase in the price of time raises the relative price of time-intensive commodities, and thereby induces substitution toward goods-intensive commodities as well as toward goods-intensive methods of producing commodities (see equation A. 20). The effect on the distribution of the observed income elasticities around their mean, and in one formulation on the relationship between the education elasticity and the observed income elasticity, depends upon the correlation between the pure income elasticity and the time-intensity of the commodities. As expenditure data become available which contain independent information on the value of time, the subsequent empirical implementation of the model will involve an important additional dimension.

As in most studies of Engel curves, the proper form of the equation is not suggested by our theory. Consequently, a number of forms were considered and no one function was unambiguously preferable to all others. The regressions were run in linear form, in double-log form for various combinations of the independent variables, and with certain cross-products or interaction effects. The form on which most emphasis was placed and for which most of the empirical results are reported below is one of the double-log forms, since this form (occasionally including some interaction effects) tended to have the highest explanatory power.[3] This conclusion of a generally superior

---

[3] It should be pointed out that this comparison is not strictly legitimate since in the linear case the residual is $u_2 = (X - \hat{X})$ and in the log case $u_1 = (\ln X - \hat{\ln} X)$; thus, the variations are in different units and the $\bar{R}^2$'s are not comparable. An adjustment is possible (but was not made here) by computing $\hat{\ln} X$, taking the antilog and correlating it with X. According to Prais and Houthakker, the adjustment "seems . . . to be of small effect for broad groups of commodities in which there are no low values" of expenditure (see S. J. Prais and H. S. Houthakker, *The Analysis of Family Budgets,* Cambridge, Cambridge University Press, 1955, p. 96).

A semilog form was not used since there appears to be little reason to presume that income elasticities fall as expenditures rise. The semilog form holds $dX/d\ln Y$ fixed, implying that $(dX_i/d\ln Y)/X_i = \eta_i$ falls as X_i rises. Now it can be argued that the elasticities may fall since the number of commodities rises as income increases. This would apply if detailed expenditure items were investigated, for higher income can lead to greater diversification in expenditures. But for the broad categories of goods studied here—clothing, travel, housing, et cetera—the increased diversification would take place within the expenditure class.

fit for a double-log form is consistent with the findings of Prais and Houthakker.[4]

Since we are interested in estimating an Engel curve for several market goods and it is clear that the separate equations in the system are not independent, we should, in principle, make use of the prior knowledge about the structure of the error terms in the system to obtain more efficient estimators. Zellner's method of estimating the whole system of equations simultaneously would seem appropriate. However, despite the fact that the disturbance terms in different equations may be correlated, this procedure collapses to a simple equation-by-equation estimation method whenever the same matrix of explanatory variables is used in each equation.[5]

A further complication arises from the fact that the model developed here suggests that the system of equations is restricted by a nonlinear constraint across the equations, involving two of the coefficients in each equation. That is, from equation (2.11.)

$$\epsilon_{iE} = K(\eta_i - 1), \qquad (3.3)$$

where ϵ_{iE} is the elasticity of expenditure on x_i with respect to education; η_i is the elasticity of expenditure on x_i with respect to income; and K is an unknown constant across all the x_i. The value of K is the estimated value of the elasticity of consumption income, ϵ_{Y_cE}. Theil develops unbiased and efficient estimators for such a system when the constraint is a linear one, and in principle the nonlinear case would be analogous to it.[6] In practice, however, the procedures used in the present study were: (1) to estimate the system, equation by equation, without imposing the constraint and then to determine the average value of the coefficient K implied by the estimates of ϵ_{iE} and η_i; and (2) to impose the constraint with an assigned value for K and, by varying the value assigned, determine that K which minimized the overall weighted residual sum of squares.

[4] After considering a linear, inverse, semilog, log-inverse, and double-log function, they conclude (ibid., p. 103), "The double-logarithmic form gives a fairly satisfactory description of the curvature found in most commodities except for the difficulty of treating zero expenditures." This latter difficulty was encountered in the data used here and was circumvented by replacing the average expenditure of zero dollars a year by an average of one dollar or one cent, as indicated.

[5] Arnold Zellner, "An Efficient Method of Estimating Seemingly Unrelated Regressions and Tests for Aggregation Bias," *Journal of the American Statistical Association*, June 1962.

[6] H. Theil, *Economic Forecasts and Policy*, Amsterdam, North-Holland Press, 1961.

THE VARIABLES CONSIDERED

The dependent variable in the Engel curves is the expenditure on the market good. The principal reason for using expenditures rather than quantities purchased is the same as in most cross-sectional studies—data on quantities purchased are generally unavailable. Family budget studies, in particular, are concerned with expenditures on various items and the apportionment of family income. Much of the empirical investigation in the following chapters is based on two such studies.

Aside from the practical consideration of availability, expenditures have two other useful properties. First, they enable us to aggregate the different goods into whatever composite seems appropriate. Second, to the extent that variations in price reflect varying quality of goods, the use of expenditures permits aggregation over various qualities and expresses the purchase in terms of some standard unit. Particularly since we are viewing the market goods as inputs in the production of commodities, and since changes in quality reflect changes in the number of some standard units of the input, these variations in quality should not be disregarded in our estimate of the commodity's income elasticity.

Using expenditures also involves some disadvantages, particularly if there are price differences that do not reflect quality variations. If such price variations are purely random they do not affect the consistency of the parameters estimated. On the other hand, if, say, prices are systematically lower in one geographical region than in another, then the inclusion of some variable that catches these price variations can increase the explanatory power of the equation and remove the effect from other independent variables. (As discussed later, there is evidence that prices are systematically lower in the Southern states than in the North and this is one rationale for the South–non-South region dummy which has been included.)

A second type of price variation can result from price dispersion in the market place. Under certain conditions these price differences may be correlated with the household's income and lead to biases in the estimate of the income effect. Mincer has shown that a search model suggests "lower prices are paid by the rich for 'luxury' goods, and by the poor for necessities." But the difficulty introduced by this relationship is not limited to the use of expenditures as the dependent variable. On the contrary, the biases discussed by Mincer exist when the dependent variable is the quantity purchased, while the bias in *expenditure* elasticities is greater the further the price elasticity is from unity.[7]

Turning to the independent variables, equally interesting and difficult problems are raised in considering the proper income measure to use in the Engel curve. Conceptually, the proper variable would be the household's long-run level of income. But one's permanent level of income, or standard of living, is related in a complex way to one's past income history, current income, and expectations about future income, so measured current income may not be the best available indicator of the household's long-run income position. Furthermore, it is well known that, if measured disposable income is used in an estimating equation as a proxy for permanent income, the income coefficient obtained is biased toward zero, and the bias is greater the larger the variance of transitory income relative to the variance of the permanent component. Also, an upward bias results in the coefficient of any other independent variable if that variable is positively correlated with permanent income.[8]

An alternative proxy for permanent income is the household's total consumption expenditure. This is commonly used since it is argued that the transitory component in expenditure is smaller than the transitory part of measured disposable income (as households attempt to smooth out their consumption expenditure by allowing savings to absorb much of the temporary fluctuation in income). Nevertheless, there are at least two difficulties in using this variable. First, under a certain specification of the model discussed by Liviatan, the use of total consumption expenditure as a proxy for permanent income involves a bias in the estimate of the true coefficient.[9] To circumvent this problem Liviatan suggests the use of a particular instrumental variable that can be shown to give a consistent estimate. Alternatively, he shows that a consistent estimate is obtained by grouping the data by measured income and using the average total consumption expenditure of each group as the independent variable. This is the method, used

[7] This model is presented in Jacob Mincer's "Market Prices, Opportunity Costs, and Income Effects," *Measurement in Economics: Studies in Mathematical Economics and Econometrics in Memory of Yehuda Grunfeld,* Palo Alto, Stanford University Press, 1963. The relevance of this search model in interpreting the estimated coefficients is discussed on p. 42.

[8] See E. Malinvaud, *Statistical Methods of Econometrics,* Chicago, Rand McNally and Company, 1966, p. 132; and Nissan Liviatan, "Errors in Variables and Engel Curve Analysis," *Econometrica,* July 1961, p. 359.

[9] N. Liviatan, "Errors in Variables and Engel Curve Analysis," p. 338.

by Liviatan himself and also suggested by Friedman, which has been followed in this study.[10]

A second difficulty with using total consumption as the independent variable involves expenditures for major durable goods. The household that purchases a durable good during the survey period—an automobile, a home, a major appliance—may be expected to exhibit a higher level of total consumption and a higher level of expenditure on that durable than it would otherwise; thus its total consumption could overstate its permanent income level and lead to an upward bias in the estimate of the income elasticity of durables. Since the estimates of the income elasticities are not independent, this could also lead to a downward biased estimate of some other items. The tendency to purchase durables with consumer credit would alleviate this problem somewhat. Also, Prais and Houthakker suggest that it "is to some extent reduced by the tendency for households to offset such expenditures by lower expenditures elsewhere."[11] Furthermore, it seems clear that the use of averages from grouped data should further reduce this problem since individual idiosyncrasies and exceptional purchases will be averaged out or possibly offset. In view of these considerations, total consumption expenditure of households (grouped by measured disposable income and other variables) was chosen as the income measure in most of the empirical work presented below. Some tests were made using measured disposable income and the Liviatan instrumental variable, but the results were not considered of sufficient interest to merit inclusion in this study. The consumption variable was, for one test, purged of durable expenditures and thus represented a more nearly pure current consumption expenditure or proxy for the total service flow from all purchased market goods; these results are given in Appendix C.

The second explanatory variable is education. Ideally, this variable would be a vector of the formal educational attainment of each family

---

[10] See N. Liviatan, *Consumption Patterns in Israel,* Jerusalem, Falk Project for Economic Research in Israel, 1964; and Milton Friedman, *A Theory of the Consumption Function,* Princeton, Princeton University Press for NBER, 1957, p. 207.

[11] They argue that given its level of total income, the household determines its expenditure on current consumption, and having made this decision proceeds to distribute this amount among the several desired goods, so that "the distribution of expenditures among the various commodities depends only on the level of total expenditure." See Prais and Houthakker, *The Analysis of Family Budgets,* p. 81. See also S. J. Prais, "A Comment," *Econometrica,* January 1959.

member, adjusted for quality and similar factors. The particular measure used here was the level of formal education of the head of the household. Presumably, there is a high correlation between the education of the head and that of other family members. However, the correlation between educational attainment of family members is not perfect and for this reason the observed relationship may be weaker than the theoretical analysis implies.

The model suggests that in order to understand household expenditure patterns one should include both permanent money income and education (or some other proxy for nonmarket productivity). But these two explanatory variables—educational attainment and, say, total consumption expenditures—are positively correlated both statistically (in one body of data, the simple correlation between $\ln C$ and $\ln E$ is $+0.59$) and in our a priori notions of what they represent, market and nonmarket productivity. Including both of these variables is intended to separate the effect of money income from the effect of nonmarket productivity.

But one might ask, "What is the intuitive sense of holding income constant and raising the education level as the multiple regression technique is intended to do, and what biases if any are introduced by this procedure?" The latter question is discussed in Appendix B. The former might be rephrased as, "Why, if two family heads have the same amount of schooling, might one household have considerably higher permanent money income?" There are a variety of possible explanations: different amounts of property income, different relative degrees of labor shortage or abundance in different occupations, different degrees of monopsony power or of union strength, different innate ability, different qualities of schooling, different amounts of on-the-job training, health or other forms of human capital, luck, and so forth. Ceteris paribus, an increase in education raises one's permanent income or one's wealth, but looking across households, that "ceteris paribus" does not hold. Permanent money income and education, though undoubtedly positively correlated, might not be highly correlated as a result of rational choices, native endowments, market conditions, or chance. The separate effects of permanent money income and nonmarket efficiency may be identified if some of these differences are operative. Appendix B explores the implications of attributing a low correlation to other differences, such as differences in ability.

The rationale for including the remaining explanatory variables—family size, age, and region—is twofold. In the first place, these variables clearly influence the household's expenditures (outlays for household durables, education, children's clothing, and sporting goods are obvious examples). So, in order to remove these influences from the income and education coefficients and to improve the explanatory power of the estimating equation, these variables deserve consideration. A more important reason for our interest in these three variables is that each may be interpreted as an additional efficiency parameter. Although the theoretical chapters of this paper were developed in terms of human capital, or education, the same basic analysis could be made for any other environmental variable which affects the productivity of the production functions.

One possible interpretation of the family-size variable is along these lines: For a group of households with the same money income, education, and age, families with more children may have less knowledge about or be less proficient in using birth control information. This may reflect a general inefficiency in acquiring and using many forms of information. By this argument, the family-size variable can be considered a proxy for the ability or inclination to obtain and make use of information, and so is negatively correlated with efficiency. The predicted direction of the effect of family size on expenditures would therefore be opposite from the predictions for education—holding money income and education fixed, an increase in family size should shift expenditures toward necessities if in fact the increase in family size reflects a decrease in efficiency.

This is not the only possible interpretation of the family-size effect in the Engel curve. One alternative is to argue that family size is an endogenous variable determined by choice, and its inclusion in the Engel curve should be given roughly the same interpretation as one would give the coefficient for, say, automobiles or any other durable good in Engel curves. That is, relative prices held fixed, one would expect positive coefficients for complements to children (or automobiles) and negative coefficients for substitutes and insignificant coefficients for all other items. Since the efficiency argument implies that luxuries will have negative family-size coefficients and necessities will have positive ones, and since this latter argument implies no correlation between η_i and the family-size coefficient, ϵ_{iF} (as long as there is no correlation between income elasticities and complementarity with children), the empirical results should distinguish between these two interpretations.

A final interpretation of the family-size variable involves the question of economies or diseconomies of scale within the household.[12]

[12] The notion of scale effects involves either shifts in the production functions of the commodities as the scale of output changes or changes in the factor prices

If increasing income and family size by the same percentage has no effect on per capita expenditures, there are no externalities of scale, and per capita expenditure and per capita income are the relevant variables for the Engel curve; if the two explanatory variables are included separately their elasticities should sum to unity in this case. This interpretation also has certain specific implications regarding the relationship of the two elasticities.[13] Whichever interpretation of the empirical findings one chooses, one may say that if expenditures shift toward necessities as family size rises, households are behaving as if their real incomes were falling; the proper explanation for this decline in real income remains an open issue.

Another efficiency parameter that has been included is the age of the head of the household. Ideally, the age of each family member should be incorporated into some age index, but in the absence of more

---

as the level of purchases changes. While it is likely, perhaps, that the scale effects differ for different commodities, the discussion here assumes the same scale effect for all commodities. This assumes away any relative price effects that would result from unequal scale effects.

Prais and Houthakker discuss these unequal "specific" scale effects in a somewhat different context. By estimating the overall economies of scale from a quality-income relationship, they infer from the separate scale parameters for each item the specific scale effects. See their *Analysis of Family Budgets*, Chapter 10.

[13] Define δ_i as the sum of η_i and ϵ_{iF}. Then if

$$\delta_i \gtrless 1 \quad \text{as} \quad \eta_i \gtrless 1,$$

per capita expenditures shift toward luxuries as incomes and family size rise proportionately, and households behave as if their real incomes rose; in this case we might say there is evidence of "economies of scale." If

$$\delta_i \lessgtr 1 \quad \text{as} \quad \eta_i \gtrless 1,$$

per capita expenditures shift toward necessities, or analogously there is evidence of "diseconomies of scale." Finally, if

$$\delta_i = 1 \quad \text{as} \quad \eta_i \gtrless 1,$$

there is no evidence of effects of scale—per capita expenditures are unaffected. These three conditions can be summarized as

$$\gamma_i = \left(\frac{-\epsilon_{iF}}{\eta_i - 1} \right) \begin{smallmatrix} \leq \\ = \\ > \end{smallmatrix} 1 \quad \text{implies} \quad \begin{smallmatrix} \text{economies of scale} \\ \text{no effects of scale} \\ \text{diseconomies of scale.} \end{smallmatrix}$$

If the latter condition does not hold with the same inequality for all commodities, we might conclude that there is no consistent evidence of any scale effects.

specific information regarding the age structure of the household the age of the head has been used. The effect of age on productivity is not unambiguous. This may be seen by considering the effect of age on one's total stock of human capital. If we believe that knowledge is acquired by experience, age may contribute to human capital through experience—a form of on-the-job training in consumption, so to speak. Experience clearly contributes information about markets, prices, and so forth and could be considered an investment in "search" to the extent the information or experience acquired at one period is relevant at some future time.

On the other hand, casual empiricism suggests that after some point one's health deteriorates with age (we observe that age-specific death rates rise and that older persons tend to have more serious and more frequent illnesses and longer periods of convalescence). Similarly, it is often suggested that the investment in human capital in the form of schooling is subject to depreciation with age.[14] Thus, while age is positively related to one form of human capital through experience, after some point it is negatively related to the stock of human capital through the depreciation rates on that stock. The average net effect of age on efficiency (or on the stock of human capital) is not clear, a priori.[15]

Finally, the region variable (a South–non-South dummy) could reflect changes in efficiency resulting from systematic differences in climate or in the quality of educational training. Here, again, the region with the higher efficiency would be expected to exhibit a systematic shift in expenditures toward luxuries. An important alternative interpretation of the region effect exists since there appear to be systematic price differences between regions, and a shift toward luxuries could be expected in the region having the relatively lower cost of living in terms of market prices.[16]

---

[14] See, for example, Yoram Ben-Porath, "The Production of Human Capital and the Life Cycle of Earnings," *Journal of Political Economy*, August 1967.

[15] Since one's wealth is the present value of an income stream over a lifetime, changes in efficiency with age do not affect one's permanent income, only the relative prices of commodities between age intervals. Thus, the predictions of the model with respect to education's effect vis-à-vis the income effects are not strictly analogous to the predicted effects of age on expenditure patterns. Ceteris paribus, if age increases efficiency, thus reducing the prices of commodities over one's lifetime, we would expect increased consumption of *commodities* with advancing age and the effect on the expenditure for goods would depend upon the substitution elasticities between periods.

[16] See Chapter 4, footnote 5.

4

An Empirical Test: The 1960 BLS Consumer Expenditures Survey

THE PRECEDING CHAPTERS have (1) set out a general framework in which one can discuss how education may be expected to affect consumption patterns of households, (2) developed certain empirical implications of this model, and (3) discussed the particular estimating equation to be used in testing these implications. We now turn to some empirical results.

The body of data discussed in this chapter is the Bureau of Labor Statistics' *Survey of Consumer Expenditures 1960–61.*[1] Published reports from this cross-sectional survey give the average expenditure of households during the year under review for various commodity groups, classified by several household characteristics. The data were grouped into cells by region (four regions), disposable income (ten groups), and years of schooling completed (four groups) for 157 observations. For each cell, the average years of schooling completed, average age of head, average family size, average yearly expenditure on each good, X_i, and the average total consumption expenditure, C, were given.

The procedure used was to fit separate Engel curves for the expenditures on various goods by the usual least-squares method. Since the observations are the cell means and the cells have an unequal number of households, the regressions are weighted by the square root of the

[1] The data were collected by personal interviews using the family or consumer unit as the unit of observation for a total of 13,728 usable observations. The sample design used in the survey is described briefly as follows in BLS Report No. 237–89: "Separate stratified area samples were selected for urban areas, rural areas in metropolitan counties, and rural areas in nonmetropolitan counties. A three-stage sample design was used within each area to obtain a sample of consumer units representative of all U.S. consumer units. . . ."

size of the cell in order to conform to the assumption of a homoscedastic residual.[2]

Before turning to the data, let us look at a simple heuristic device that is useful in determining the extent to which the data are broadly consistent with the neutrality model of Chapter 2. The neutrality model suggests that the effect of education on expenditures will be positive, zero, or negative as the income elasticity is greater than, equal to, or less than unity. There are, then, nine possible combinations of the two coefficients, three of which are consistent with the neutrality model. This may be summarized by a two-way schematic diagram relating the estimated income elasticities and education elasticities. In this diagram those cells on one diagonal (the cells containing x's) are consistent with education having a positive, technologically neutral effect on nonmarket productivity. If, for example, the income elasticity of some good were 0.75 and statistically less than unity and its educa-

Education Elasticity   *Income Elasticity*

	$\eta > 1$	$\eta \simeq 1$	$\eta < 1$
$\epsilon_E > 0$	x		
$\epsilon_E \simeq 0$		x	
$\epsilon_E < 0$			x

[2] Assume the error term u in the ungrouped individual data is a random variable distributed independently of the determining variables and has an expected value of zero and a variance σ^2. Then the variance of the error term in the grouped data, $\sigma_{\bar{u}}^2$ is inversely proportional to the size of the cell n_i:

$$\sigma_{\bar{u}}^2 = \sigma^2/n.$$

Weighting by the square root of the cell size, $\sqrt{n_i}$, restores the homoscedasticity:

$$\bar{u}' = (\sqrt{n_i}u_1 + \sqrt{n_i}u_2 + \ldots + \sqrt{n_i}u_n)/n_i$$
$$\text{var}(\bar{u}') = \text{var}[\sqrt{n_i}(u_1 + u_2 + \ldots + u_n)/n_i]$$
$$= n_i(n_i \text{ var}(u))/n_i^2 = \text{var}(u).$$

All regressions across cell means in this study are so weighted. For a more thorough discussion of weighted regressions, see Malinvaud, *Statistical Methods,* pp. 242–46.

tion elasticity 0.30 and statistically significant, that good would fall into the upper right-hand cell and would not be consistent with a positive, neutral effect. On the basis of a purely random selection—no relationship between the two elasticities—one would expect one-third of the expenditure items to fall along this diagonal. Notice that even those items on the principal diagonal, or conforming in signs, need not imply strict neutrality; the latter would require a constant ratio between ϵ_E and $(\eta - 1)$ (see equation 2.11).

THE GOODS-SERVICES DICHOTOMY

The expenditure items were first aggregated into two categories, goods and services, where the differentiation was made principally on the intuitive grounds of the tangibility of the product. The "goods" component included expenditures on food for home consumption, tobacco, alcohol, shelter, utilities, housefurnishings and equipment, clothing, reading, and automobiles (purchases and operation expenses). The "service" component included expenditures for food away from home, household operations, personal care, medical care, recreation, education, and travel expenses other than automobile. The results of these two regressions on the 157 observations using the log of expenditure as the dependent variable are given below (*t* values are in parentheses).

Item	ln Consumption	ln Education	Age	Family Size	Region	$\bar{R}^2$
Goods	0.934 (65.66)	−0.073 (−4.28)	−0.003 (−4.75)	0.026 (2.54)	−0.045 (−6.52)	.996
Services	1.117 (41.86)	0.189 (5.93)	0.006 (4.68)	−0.048 (−2.54)	0.101 (7.77)	.988

The income elasticity of "goods" is 0.934, significantly less than unity, and, as predicted, the education coefficient is negative; the income elasticity of "services" is greater than one and, also as predicted, its education coefficient is positive. The interpretation of these results in the context of the model developed in the earlier chapters is that, as the education level rose, nonmarket productivity was increased, contributing to the household's real income. This additional real income was allocated between the two commodities on the basis of their income elasticities. Thus, the consumption of services rose relative to the consumption of goods, and, since the productivity effect was presumed to be neutral, this resulted in an increase in the expenditure on services and a decrease in the expenditure on goods.

There was a tradeoff of "goods" inputs for "services" inputs, and the weighted average of the two education effects was zero (or, more precisely, 0.001).

The table discussed above illustrates the consistency of these results with the predictions of the model. Both of the expenditure items fall on the principal diagonal. One should keep in mind when evaluating the results for this dichotomy that since the weighted average of the consumption elasticities (or income elasticities) must be unity and the weighted average of the education elasticities must be zero, there is in fact only one degree of freedom in the two regressions for each coefficient.[3]

Education Elasticity	Income Elasticity		
	$\eta > 1$	$\eta \simeq 1$	$\eta < 1$
$\epsilon_E > 0$	Services		
$\epsilon_E \simeq 0$			
$\epsilon_E < 0$			Goods

The family-size coefficients show a relative increase in expenditures for goods over services as size increases (holding constant the household's income, education, age, and region as these variables are defined). So, ceteris paribus, an increase in family size shifts expenditures toward necessities, or the larger families behave as if they had lower real income. Any of the three explanations discussed in Chapter 3 can offer an interpretation: "Goods" may be on balance more complementary with children; larger families may be less efficient and thus in fact have lower real incomes; or, since $-\epsilon_{iF}/(\eta_i - 1) > 1$ for

---

[3] For example, given that ϵ_{gE} for goods is -0.073 and its weight is 72.7 per cent, by deduction ϵ_{sE} for services is:

$$\epsilon_{gE}w_g + \epsilon_{sE}w_s = 0$$
$$-0.073\,(0.727) + \epsilon_{sE}\,(0.273) = 0$$
$$\epsilon_{sE} = +0.19 .$$

both goods and services, the evidence is consistent with some diseconomies of scale.[4]

The age coefficients suggest that households with older heads, ceteris paribus, spend a larger share of their expenditures on services. Of all the ad hoc explanations, the most appealing seems to be that since the goods component includes purchases of consumer durables and housing, this age effect is simply reflecting the fact that households tend to purchase these durable items at a younger age.

The relatively strong effect of the region dummy is intriguing. If interpreted as an efficiency. parameter, it suggests that living in the South, other things being the same, increases efficiency. Unfortunately, it is not clear what effect the variable is reflecting. It might be the effect of climate, or the degree of urbanization, but, alternatively, it could be differences in prices.[5] If prices are systematically lower in the South, since the multiple regression holds total consumption expenditures fixed, a household in the South would be purchasing a larger basket of goods; that is, it would have a higher real income. If this is the case, the Southern household would be expected to shift .its consumption pattern towards luxuries—as in fact it appears to do.

As in the case of the more detailed expenditure classification presented in the latter part of this chapter, the Engel curves for goods and services were fitted in a number of forms. The linear fit for the two categories is shown below (with t values in parentheses).

The expenditure item "shelter" includes expenditures for rent and

	Consumption	Education	Age	Family Size	Region	$\bar{R}^2$
Goods	58.882 (56.19)	−3.570 (−0.46)	−5.159 (−1.56)	248.144 (6.30)	−207.188 (−7.52)	.993
Mean Elasticity	.828	−0.010				
Services	35.417 (44.95)	11.679 (2.01)	5.194 (2.09)	−176.330 (−5.96)	172.026 (8.31)	.982
Mean Elasticity	1.326	0.088				

[4] See Chapter 3, footnote 13. The mean family-size elasticities of the two items are:

$$\epsilon_{gF} = +0.083$$
$$\epsilon_{sF} = -0.154;$$

thus

$$-\epsilon_{iF}/(\eta_i - 1) = 1.26 \text{ and } 1.32, \text{ respectively.}$$

[5] The Department of Labor estimates an index of comparative living costs of city workers. The simple average for ten metropolitan areas and one nonmetro-

repairs by renters and expenditures for mortgage interest payments, property taxes, and insurance and repairs by homeowners, plus other lodging expenditures. Since the forgone return on the owner's equity and the repayment of the mortgage principal are not included, the shelter expenditure does not adequately reflect the household's consumption of the item, and biased estimates result if the percentage of homeowners varies systematically across cells. The shelter item was therefore adjusted to reflect more adequately changes in expenditure across the cells. The total consumption expenditure (the independent variable) was also adjusted to reflect total current consumption expenditure, C^*.[6] The results of the comparable regressions using H_R in the goods component and using C^* are (with t values in parentheses):

Item	ln Consumption*	ln Education	Age	Family Size	Region	$\bar{R}^2$
Goods	0.957	−0.120	−0.007	0.004	−0.032	.993
	(45.82)	(−4.94)	(−7.01)	(2.89)	(−3.23)	
Partial Correlation	0.97	−0.38	−0.51	0.24	−0.26	
Services	1.165	0.144	0.001	−0.002	0.128	.989
	(39.78)	(4.25)	(0.40)	(−1.33)	(9.39)	
Partial Correlation	0.96	0.34	0.03	−0.11	0.62	

It is interesting to note that, in addition to increasing the significance of the predicted education effect on both items, the use of C^* emphasizes

politan area in the South was an index of 93 compared to 102 in the non-South for twenty-nine metropolitan areas and three regional nonmetropolitan areas for autumn 1966. Similar indices of 94 and 101 in autumn 1959 for goods, rents, and services in four cities in the South and sixteen cities in the non-South suggest that market prices are lower in the South. See Helen H. Lamale and M.S. Stotz, "The Interim City Worker's Family Budget," *Monthly Labor Review*, August 1960.

[6] Since Shelter $= H_O + H_r + H_D$, i.e., the sum of housing expenditure by owners (o) and renters (r) and other dwelling expenditures, the new housing variable H_R was defined as

$$H_R = \frac{(\text{Shelter} - H_O - H_D)}{\text{per cent } R} + H_D,$$

where per cent R is the fraction of households in the cell that rent their homes. Thus, H_R is considered an estimate of what the rental figure would be if all households in the cell were renters. The H_D is predominantly "lodging out of home city." Since H_R is undefined for cells with no renters, of which there were nine in the 157 total, regressions using H_R in any form had 148 observations.

Total current consumption is defined as

$$C^* = C - \text{Shelter} - \text{housefurnishings} - \text{automobile} + H_R.$$

Again, all regressions using this variable contain 148 observations, since H_R is undefined where the cell contains no renters.

the fact that age is an important determinant of expenditures for durables (included in the goods component) but not of expenditures for nondurable services.

THE CONSUMPTION PATTERN

To go beyond this broad dichotomization of expenditures, similar weighted regressions were run for each of the following detailed items: food at home, food away from home, tobacco, alcohol, housing,[7] utilities, household operations, housefurnishings and equipment, clothing, medical care, personal care, leisure (reading and recreation), education, and travel. The regression equations for these fourteen market goods are given in Table 1.

TABLE 1

Regression Equations for Consumption Items, 1960 BLS Data,
Constant Elasticities

Item	ln Consumption	ln Education	Age	Family Size	Region	$\bar{R}^2$
Food (home)	0.639 (14.07)	−0.173 (−3.18)	0.001 (0.50)	0.141 (4.40)	−0.133 (−5.78)	.939
Food (away)	1.225 (16.09)	0.205 (2.25)	0.002 (0.63)	−0.099 (−1.85)	0.078 (2.09)	.927
Tobacco	0.723 (5.32)	−0.852 (−5.24)	−0.034 (−5.08)	0.0349 (0.36)	−0.0436 (−0.66)	.702
Alcohol	1.611 (13.06)	−0.584 (−3.95)	−0.024 (−3.84)	−0.214 (−2.46)	−0.576 (−9.55)	.899
Housing	1.008 (17.77)[a]	0.3767 (5.56)	0.0201 (7.12)	−0.1028 (−2.58)	−0.1268 (−4.64)	.937
Utilities	0.435 (7.54)	0.126 (1.82)	0.013 (4.52)	0.179 (4.40)	−0.126 (−4.47)	.851
Household operations	1.113 (30.54)	0.314 (7.19)	0.008 (4.14)	−0.086 (−3.35)	0.183 (10.28)	.978
Housefurnishings and equipment	0.981 (13.30)[a]	−0.059 (−0.67)	−0.008 (−2.09)	0.167 (3.20)	0.118 (3.27)	.938
Clothing	1.216 (28.63)	−0.024 (−0.48)	−0.005 (−2.38)	0.078 (2.62)	0.108 (5.20)	.982
Personal care	0.939 (24.90)	−0.125 (−2.75)	−0.010 (−5.36)	0.000 (0.02)	0.159 (8.62)	.974
Medical care	0.831 (13.04)	0.030 (0.39)	0.00 (2.50)	0.01 (0.24)	0.033 (1.06)	.888
Leisure	1.299 (25.58)	0.147 (2.41)	−0.007 (−2.81)	−0.030 (−0.83)	−0.062 (−2.48)	.977
Education	1.594 (7.26)	1.485 (5.64)	0.021 (1.94)	0.505 (3.26)	0.431 (4.02)	.877
Travel	1.386 (18.62)	−0.416 (−4.67)	−0.029 (−7.76)	−0.028 (−0.53)	0.075 (2.06)	.957

Note: *t* values in parentheses.
[a] Implies coefficient not statistically different from one (the *t* values for testing the difference from unity are 0.14 for housing and −0.26 for housefurnishings).

---

[7] "Housing" is defined here as the ratio of total shelter expenditures minus expenditures for owned dwellings to the percentage of households that rent.

To consider the relationship between the income elasticities and the sign of the education coefficients, we again make use of our two-way schematic diagram.

Education Elasticity	Income Elasticity		
	$\eta > 1$	$\eta \simeq 1$	$\eta < 1$
$\epsilon_E > 0$	Food away Household operations Leisure Education	Housing	Utilities
$\epsilon_E \simeq 0$	Clothing	Housefurnishings and equipment	Medical care
$\epsilon_E < 0$	Alcohol Travel		Food at home Tobacco Personal care

Eight of these items are qualitatively consistent with the neutrality model for education. Food away from home, household operations, leisure, and education expenditures are luxuries and have positive education effects; food at home, tobacco, and personal care are necessities and have negative education coefficients, as predicted. The income elasticity for housefurnishings and equipment is approximately 1.0 and, as expected, the effect of education on this item is negligible. The housing item is consistent in terms of sign, but the income elasticity is not statistically different from unity.

The remaining five items—utilities, travel, clothing, medical expenditures, and alcohol—are not consistent with the neutrality model. The first point that should be made regarding these items is that, while the simple neutrality model developed in Chapter 2 is not suitable for interpreting these results, the basic model of Chapter 1 is. For example, if we believe that education's effect on the production function that uses clothing as an input is less than its effect on other production functions—and is positive in general—then the relative price of commodity Z_c would rise, $(\widetilde{\Pi}_c - \widetilde{\Pi}) > 0$. Thus, even though the income elasticity is greater than unity, the increase in the relative price could induce enough substitution away from Z_c to offset the income effect.[8] So the insignificant education effect may be viewed as the net

[8] The equation in Chapter 2, footnote 7 is useful here. We have seen that for clothing $\eta_i > 1$; thus, the first term, the income effect, would be positive. If we

effect of the expansion from the income effect and the contraction caused by a change in the relative price of Z_c. In a similar manner, any other item not consistent with the simple neutrality model may also be reflecting a nonneutral productivity effect of education.

This explanation has a shortcoming: it is conjectural. Since we do not know the direction of the technological bias or the size of the price elasticity of the commodity, the explanation of the nonneutral case can only be offered ex post. The model can interpret the nonneutral cases but we cannot form expectations about them. Thus, its predictive power is impaired by the existence of nonneutrality. However, the model is still useful in helping us understand these expenditure patterns, and, from a broader perspective, the essence of the model itself leads us to expect relative price effects even though we are as yet unable to specify where they may be strongest. As more relevant data become available and as additional evidence is accumulated, the basic model of Chapter 1 will allow us to interpret these nonneutral cases, incorporating substitution effects as well as changes in income.[9] For the present, the formulation is restricted to the joint hypothesis that education has a positive effect on nonmarket production and that this effect is neutral across items.

Nevertheless, a few of these nonneutral cases deserve some special attention. Consider the alcohol expenditure. Grossman argues that in addition to being an input in the production of some desirable commodity associated with alcoholic beverages, alcohol is also a *negative* input in the production of "good health."[10] So, if additional education

suppose $(\tilde{\Pi}_i - \tilde{\Pi}) > 0$ and $|\epsilon_i| > 1$, the substitution effect will be negative and could offset the positive income effect. So if education is biased away from Z_c, and Z_c is price-elastic, $\bar{x}_i$ may be zero as observed. Alternatively, if education is biased toward Z_c and it is price-inelastic, the substitution effect could again offset the income effect.

A third alternative, consistent with this item and with the observed coefficients for housefurnishings and medical care, is that $Y_c = 0$, that is, education has no consumption income effect.

[9] From the equation mentioned in the previous footnote it is clear that, ceteris paribus, we would expect larger price effects for items whose price elasticities are farther from minus unity. In the recent literature showing various estimates of price elasticities for broad categories of expenditure, such a relationship between ϵ_i and nonneutrality is at best only faintly observable. Most of these price elasticity estimates indicate inelasticity. If we believe that all of these items are price-inelastic, we would infer that education is biased toward those items below the principal diagonal in the two-way diagram above.

[10] See M. Grossman, "The Demand for Health."

increases the demand for good health through an income effect, one way this commodity might be increased is by substitution away from alcohol. This could explain the negative effect of education on alcohol expenditures.[11]

Since the expenditure on travel includes the purchase of an automobile, this item is particularly vulnerable to the bias discussed in Appendix B relating to durable goods.[12] The direction of this bias was shown to be upward for the income elasticity and downward for the education coefficient or any independent variable positively related to consumption. Such a bias could help explain the finding for travel, that its income elasticity is 1.39 and its education elasticity is −0.42. To the extent that clothing is a durable good the argument also applies to that item.[13]

Finally, it is possible to offer another explanation for some observed nonneutrality. This explanation relies on the search model mentioned in the previous chapter. Mincer has shown that the existence of price dispersion in markets for consumer goods will, under certain conditions, result in wealthier consumers paying relatively lower prices for luxuries and relatively higher prices for necessities.[14] If it were assumed that education had no nonmarket productivity effect, and that nonwage income (V) were zero, then changes in education would have the same proportionate effect on income and on the price of

---

[11] The argument might be applied to tobacco consumption as well. In this case, however, the negative education effect observed is also consistent with the commodity being a necessity.

[12] The fact that this bias is stronger for durable goods leads Prais and Houthakker to qualify their conclusions that consumption is the preferable determining variable in Engel curves by saying it "seems preferable a priori, at any rate for those items that are not household durables." See Prais and Houthakker, *The Analysis of Family Budgets*, p. 81.

[13] Regarding expenditures on housing, Margaret Reid, in her study on housing and income, concludes, "Estimates . . . indicate an elasticity of housing with respect to normal (permanent) income close to 2.0." See Margaret Reid, *Housing and Income*, Chicago, University of Chicago Press, 1962, p. 377. This suggests that the results I obtained here considerably understate the income effect; if such a bias exists, it will likewise overstate the effect of education on housing expenditures, which can explain the findings shown here vis-à-vis the neutrality model.

[14] See J. Mincer, "Market Prices, Opportunity Costs, and Income Effects," p. 80. I am grateful to Jacob Mincer for several conversations from which this discussion emerged.

time. If, then, all commodities had the same time intensity, in the context of Mincer's search model the more educated would pay lower prices for luxuries and the less educated would pay lower prices for necessities.

Thus, in a multiple regression that holds total consumption expenditure (but not income) constant, if all items are price-elastic, education would be expected to have a positive effect on expenditures for luxuries and a negative effect on necessities. This is the same predicted effect as the positive neutral nonmarket-productivity hypothesis implies. On the other hand, if all items are price-inelastic, education would be negatively correlated with expenditures on luxuries and positively correlated with expenditures for necessities.[15]

This discussion of the search model emphasizes two important points. First, if differences in the price of time and market search are partly captured by the education variable, price effects may result which will induce some substitution. The influence of education on the efficiency of search in general is a part of its nonmarket productivity effect. But differences in the price of time which induce shifts in the relative amounts of search are not. Second, without relying on the concept of nonmarket productivity one can develop other models that will generate the same implications about the observed effects of education. But these models—one that relies on search costs, for example, or one that assumes education affects the utility function directly (see Appendix A)—require sets of assumptions which are quite strong and surely not innocuous. They also appear to be no more capable of predicting the nonneutral cases than the nonmarket productivity model.

---

[15] A difficulty with this interpretation arises when we consider the additional explanatory variable, C, total consumption expenditure. If income rises as education rises (with C held fixed), then C is an inadequate measure of permanent income. Indeed, given the assumptions of the previous paragraph, C can be interpreted as reflecting only transitory changes in income.

An alternative set of assumptions would be to allow $V > 0$ and to suggest that the wage and V are negatively related—as E raises the wage (and the price of time), V declines. Then, holding C fixed, the increase in E involves a compensated rise in the wage and little or no change in income. In the simple but extreme case where income is completely unaffected, the rise in E would reduce search and thereby raise all prices absolutely, affect no relative prices, and lead to a reduction in the real value of the market basket and thus to a relative shift toward necessities.

Before leaving Table 1, let us briefly consider the coefficients of the other independent variables.[16] Looking at the results with respect to the age variable, one gets the impression that the age effect has again duplicated the education results. In only two of the fourteen cases (food at home and leisure) do the signs of the education and age coefficients differ. But the following diagram suggests how infrequently the age variable shifted expenditures toward luxuries.

Age Effect		*Income Elasticities*	
	$\eta > 1$	$\eta \simeq 1$	$\eta < 1$
(+)	Household operations Education	Housing	Utilities Medical care
(0)	Food away		Food at home
(−)	Alcohol Clothing Leisure Travel	Housefurnish- ings and equipment	Tobacco Personal care

In fact, the diagram suggests that, despite its apparent similarity to the education effect, the age effect is quite erratic. (Note that the effect of age on the consumer durable items is negative.)

Regarding the family-size coefficients, an intuitively satisfying interpretation of many of these results is that items complementary to children—probably food, housefurnishings and equipment, utilities, clothing, and education—have significant positive effects, while the more substitutable items—perhaps alcohol and food away from home —have negative effects, with some other items exhibiting no significant effects whatever.[17] The hypothesis that, other things held constant, an increase in family size reflects a decrease in nonmarket efficiency and so leads to a shift toward necessities is consistent with twelve of these items (clothing and education are the exceptions), although only five exhibit statistical significance.

[16] Some caution is necessary in interpreting these age and family-size effects since the data were not cross-classified by these two variables and only the cell means are used. On balance this introduces no biases but does cause an understatement of the statistical significance of the coefficients. For a discussion of this point, see Yoel Haitovsky, "Unbiased Multiple Regression Coefficients," *Journal of the American Statistical Association,* September 1966.

[17] From the vantage point of my personal intuition, the exceptions here are that household operations and housing appear to be substitutes while medical care and travel are not significantly affected by family size.

Viewing family size as a scale phenomenon, it was suggested in Chapter 3 that a γ_i (defined in Chapter 3, footnote 13) greater than unity for all items implies diseconomies of scale, while a γ_i less than unity implies economies of scale. Alternatively, one might look at δ_i, the sum of the income- and family-size elasticities, as the degree of homogeneity of the function with respect to income and family size. Table 2 gives the value of γ_i and δ_i for each item (γ_i is undefined for $\eta_i = 1$ and therefore is not reported for two items, housing and housefurnishings). The figures in the table do not constitute evidence of either economies or diseconomies of scale.[18]

TABLE 2
Implied Scale Effects of Family Size, by Item

Item	γ_i	δ_i	Item	γ_i	δ_i
Food (home)	1.25	1.09	Housefurnishings and equipment		1.52
Food (away)	1.41	0.91	Clothing	−1.16	1.47
Tobacco	0.40	0.84	Personal care	0.05	0.94
Alcohol	1.12	0.93	Medical care	0.21	0.87
Housing		0.68	Leisure	0.42	1.20
Utilities	1.04	1.01	Education	−2.72	3.21
Household operations	2.44	0.84	Travel	0.23	1.30

The effect of region on real income is also more difficult to determine for these detailed expenditure items. For eight of the fourteen, the coefficient is consistent with the hypothesis that real income is higher in the South (i.e., expenditures shift toward luxuries), but for the remaining six items, Southerners shifted expenditures toward necessities. The conclusion at this point must be that the mechanism through which region affects expenditures and the direction of its effect on real income remain open questions.

These same regressions were run in linear form, and the results are summarized in Table 3. One can compare these elasticities with those shown in Table 1. All of these linear regressions include the

[18] One cannot conclude from this evidence that there are no important scale effects. One circumstance that could produce the results observed would be unequal scale effects for the various commodities. For example, in Chapter 10 of their *Analysis of Family Budgets,* Prais and Houthakker suggest that the specific economies of scale in foodstuffs are about +.2 while their overall estimate of economies of scale is about +.13. So as size increases, foodstuffs become relatively cheaper. Thus, the observed relative shift toward food at home as income and family size increase proportionately may be reflecting substitution toward that relatively cheaper commodity; it need not imply diseconomies of scale. Only if there were a consistent shift toward necessities might one infer something about overall economies of scale.

TABLE 3
Elasticity Estimates, Linear Form

Item	$\bar{\eta}_i$	$\bar{\epsilon}_{iE}$	$\bar{\epsilon}_{iF}$	$\bar{R}^2$	Mean Expenditure
Food (home)	0.526	−0.112	0.554	.9496	989
Food (away)	1.455	−0.021	−0.606	.8988	246
Tobacco	0.519	−0.563	0.224	.8176	91
Alcohol	1.455	−0.349	−0.397	.8375	78
Housing	1.832	−0.094	−1.458	.6718	658
Utilities	0.463	0.052	0.450	.8850	249
Household operations	1.493	0.198	−0.808	.9204	288
Housefurnishings and equipment	1.028	0.043	0.246	.9233	266
Clothing	1.338	−0.054	−0.026	.9761	518
Personal care	0.855	−0.136	0.034	.9634	145
Medical care	0.893	−0.027	−0.106	.8669	340
Leisure	1.221	0.298	0.041	.9602	245
Education	2.787	1.262	−1.176	.6937	53
Automobiles	0.938	−0.146	0.319	.8869	693
Travel (not auto)	2.167	−0.169	−1.308	.4897	77
Weighted average[a]	1.1036	−0.0467	−0.1221		

[a] See text for a discussion of these averages.

same set of five independent variables: total consumption, education, age, family size, and region. The weighted averages of η_i and ϵ_{iE} do not equal unity or zero in this case, since the housing Engel curve has fewer observations than the other regressions and therefore is not strictly consistent with the other fourteen items. When including the consistent "shelter" item and also fitting the equation to the remaining "miscellaneous expenditures" item, the weighted average of the η_i is 1.0000 and of the ϵ_{iE}, −0.0002.

In order to determine whether there were interaction effects between some of the independent variables, many of the Engel curves were also run in double-log form, while the cross-products of total consumption with education and of total consumption with age were included as separate independent variables. Thus, the equation fitted was

$$\ln X = a + b_1 \ln C + b_2 \ln E + b_3 A + b_4 F + b_5 R + b_6$$
$$(\ln C \cdot \ln E) + b_7 [\ln C \cdot (A)] + \epsilon , \qquad (4.1)$$

and the income elasticity varies in this case with the level of education and age (provided b_6 and/or b_7 is not zero). The income elasticity at the mean is defined as

$$\bar{\eta}_i = \frac{\partial \ln X_i}{\partial \ln C} = b_1 + b_6 \overline{\ln E} + b_7 \bar{A}. \qquad (4.2)$$

So, for instance, if b_7 is positive, the income elasticity rises with age.

Table 4 shows the implied elasticities of income, education, and family size from the "best" regression (in terms of highest $\bar{R}^2$) in the various forms fitted. The "constant" form gives a constant income and

TABLE 4

Elasticity Estimates, Form With Highest $\bar{R}^2$

Item	η_i	ϵ_{iE}	ϵ_{iF}	$\bar{R}^2$ [a]	Form[b]	Mean Expenditure[c]
Food (home)	0.526	−0.112	0.554	.950	1	989
Food (away)	1.225	0.205	−0.319	.927	2	246
Tobacco	0.519	−0.563	0.224	.818	1	91
Alcohol	1.611	−0.584	−0.687	.899	2	78
Housing	0.990	0.372	−0.397	.942	3	658
Utilities	0.463	0.052	0.450	.885	1	249
Household operations	1.113	0.314	−0.277	.978	2	288
Housefurnishings and equipment	0.981	−0.059	0.536	.938	2	266
Clothing	1.113	0.083	0.377	.984	3	518
Personal care	0.939	−0.125	0.002	.974	2	145
Medical care	0.831	0.030	0.034	.888	2	340
Leisure	1.299	0.147	−0.096	.977	2	245
Education	1.594	1.485	1.622	.877	2	53
Automobiles	1.228	−0.347	0.290	.938	3	693
Travel (not auto)	1.378	0.097	−0.831	.802	3	77
Weighted average	0.9517	0.0186	0.1532			
Simple average	1.054	0.0663	0.0988			

[a] See footnote 3, Chapter 3.
[b] Form: 1 = linear; 2 = constant elasticity; 3 = interaction.
[c] Mean total expenditure = 4936.

education elasticity; all others are computed at the mean value of the relevant variables. The "interaction" form is that shown in equation (4.1). The relationship between ϵ_{iE} and η_i is summarized in the following two-way diagram and is also illustrated in Chart 1.

Education Elasticity	Income Elasticity	
	$\eta > 1$	$\eta < 1$
$\epsilon_E > 0$	Food away Household operations Clothing Leisure Education Travel (not auto)	Housing Utilities Medical care
$\epsilon_E < 0$	Alcohol Automobiles	Food at home Tobacco Housefurnishings Personal care

CHART 1

Scatter Diagram of the Income and Education Elasticities,
Fifteen Observations

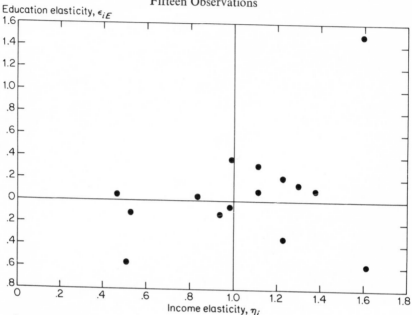

SOURCE: Table 4.

THE IMPLIED CONSUMPTION INCOME ELASTICITY

From the evidence summarized in Table 4, the neutrality model is consistent with two-thirds of the consumption items, or 60 per cent of total expenditure. (Chart 1 suggests that another 25 per cent of total expenditures—housing, utilities, and medical care—is not far outside the "neutral" quadrants I and III.) Since the model implies a positive relationship between the education and income elasticities, the correlation between ϵ_{iE} and η_i (or $\eta_i - 1$) should be positive. The simple correlation for the data in Table 4 is 0.366, with a weighted correlation of 0.176; the former is a simple average over the separate items, while the latter is equivalent to a simple average over each dollar of expenditure. The relationship in both cases has the expected sign.

Equation (2.11) suggests that the ratio of ϵ_{iE} to $(\eta_i - 1)$ is an estimate of the elasticity of consumption income, ϵ_{Y_cE}. Since each separate regression gives an estimate of ϵ_{Y_cE}, the average estimate could be considered a measure of ϵ_{Y_cE} over all expenditure items. The simple and weighted averages of ϵ_{Y_cE} across the items are $+0.644$ and $+0.274$, respectively, where the weights are expenditure shares and the averages exclude housing and personal care, since ϵ_{Y_cE} is not defined when $\eta = 1$.[19] Here, too, the relationship appears to be positive and the elasticity of consumption income is estimated to be between one-quarter and two-thirds.

An alternative procedure for estimating ϵ_{Y_cE} is to regress ϵ_{iE} on $(\eta_i - 1)$. Using each of the fifteen pairs of estimates of the income and education elasticities from Table 4, a regression of the form

$$\epsilon_{iE} = b(\eta_i - 1) + e_i \tag{4.3}$$

was run, weighting by expenditure shares and forcing the intercept to be zero. The observed regression slope, b, is an estimate of ϵ_{Y_cE}, the elasticity of consumption income with respect to education. The regression coefficient is $+0.084$ (its t value is 0.43); in unweighted form the estimated coefficient is $+0.490$ (1.47). These regression estimates are not statistically significant; the point estimates suggest that a percentage increase in the level of education raises real full income by about one-tenth of a per cent (or one-half a per cent if the unweighted regression estimate is used). That is, as education rises, with the household's permanent money income held fixed, on the average the composition of expenditures shifts toward luxuries, and the magnitude of that shift implies that a percentage increase in education is equivalent to a tenth of a percentage increase in income. This estimate of the magnitude of consumption income elasticity is quite small and its standard error relatively large. Other estimates, using different combinations of the Engel curves presented here, are discussed in Appendix C.[20] Overall, the value of the consumption income elasticity appears to be positive, though small, but this should not be considered more than a very tentative conclusion.

A final procedure used to estimate the elasticity of consumption income is to impose the neutrality assumption on the system of equa-

[19] For the goods-services dichotomy in the first section of this chapter, ϵ_{Y_cE}: services, 1.615; goods, 1.106; unweighted average, 1.36; weighted average, 1.24.

[20] Appendix C, section 6, discusses this regression procedure in greater detail and presents other slope coefficients. Because of the problem of biases related to durable goods, the elasticity of consumption income was estimated from the nondurables alone; in the weighted form its value was $+0.496$ (t value $= 3.75$).

tions and to estimate the magnitude of the neutral effect of education on nonmarket productivity by an iterative technique. Using the function for expenditure item X_i

$$\ln X_i = a_i + \eta_i \ln C + \epsilon_{iE} \ln E + b_{3i}A + b_{4i}F + b_{5i}R + e_i , \quad (4.4)$$

we can substitute the neutrality constraint (from equation 3.3)

$$\epsilon_{iE} = K(\eta_i - 1)$$

into the expenditure function, and obtain

$$(\ln X_i + K \ln E) = a_i + \eta_i (\ln C + K \ln E) + b_{3i}A \\ + b_{4i}F + b_{5i}R + e_i . \quad (4.5)$$

This equation was estimated for various assigned values of K. For each K the residual sum of squares was summed over the expenditure items; Table 5 indicates the overall sums of squares weighted by ex-

TABLE 5

Overall Residual Sums of Squares, by Values of the Elasticity of Consumption Income K

Value of K	Overall Residual Sum of Squares	Value of K	Overall Residual Sum of Squares
−1.00	4.144	0.65	3.379
−0.25	3.555	0.75	3.379
0.00	3.449	0.85	3.381
0.10	3.424	1.00	3.421
0.25	3.399	3.00	3.458
0.50	3.381	10.00	3.551
0.55	3.380		

penditure shares. The value of K that yields the smallest weighted sum of squares is in the vicinity of 0.65 to 0.75, which is considerably larger than the other estimates of the elasticity of consumption income just presented.[21]

From an analysis of the residual variance in Table 5, an F value is computed which suggests that an estimate of K in the range of 0.65 or 0.75 is a statistically significant improvement over a value for K of zero. Although the residual sums of squares in the table do not vary greatly in magnitude, the reduction of about two per cent, given

[21] For consistency, these estimates, derived from imposing various values of K, all contain only 148 observations, since the housing variable was not defined for cells in which there were no renters. Also, the same double-log form with no interaction effects was used for all fourteen items, so these results are not precisely comparable with those using the form with the highest adjusted-R^2. (There were fourteen items used here since "travel" and "automobile" were combined into one item.)

the large number of degrees of freedom, is significant. The variation appears to be sufficient to suggest with some confidence that this iterative procedure places the value of K above zero and above the previous estimate of one-tenth.[22]

Table 5 also permits a test of the neutrality assumption itself. Since this iterative procedure imposes the neutrality constraint on the system of demand equations while the equation-by-equation estimation does not, the overall residual sums of squares in the two cases can be compared. The analysis of variance suggests that neutrality is imposed at a high cost in terms of the residual variation: the effect of education appears to be nonneutral.[23] As was stressed repeatedly in Chapter 2,

[22] I wish to thank Finis Welch for suggesting this test to me. See Marvin Kosters and Finis Welch, "The Effect of Minimum Wages on the Distribution of Changes in Aggregate Employment," forthcoming in *American Economic Review*. From Table 5, the residual sum of squares from imposing the neutrality constraint with $K = 0.0$ is 3.449 and the total degrees of freedom are $2002 = 14(148 - 4 - 1)$. By iteration over various values of K the residual variation is reduced to 3.379 at a value of $K = 0.65$. So by selecting that value of K, one degree of freedom is lost and the residual variation is lowered by $0.070 = (3.449 - 3.379)$. Thus,

$$F_{1,2001} = \frac{0.070/1}{3.379/2001} = 41.46 .$$

Following Kosters-Welch a step further, since this F test has degrees of freedom (1,2001), the square root of F has a t distribution. If we suppose

$$\sqrt{F_{1,2001}} = t \approx \frac{\hat{K} - 0}{\sigma_{\hat{K}}},$$

we can obtain an estimate of the standard error of K (for $K = 0.65$) as

$$\hat{\sigma}_{\hat{K}} = \frac{\hat{K}}{\sqrt{F_{1,2001}}} = \frac{0.65}{6.44} = 0.101 ,$$

or, for $K = 0.75$,

$$\hat{\sigma}_{\hat{K}} = \frac{0.75}{6.44} = 0.116,$$

which suggests that the estimated value of K at 0.65 or 0.75 has an estimated standard error of about 0.11.

[23] Estimating equation (4.4) for all fourteen items separately for the 148 observations gives $14(148-5-1) = 1988$ degrees of freedom, and the observed overall weighted residual sum of squares is 2.660. By imposing the neutrality model, one fewer parameter is estimated per equation, while one degree of freedom is lost by choosing the value of K which minimizes the overall weighted residual sum of squares. So the degrees of freedom in the constrained case is $14(148 - 4 - 1) - 1 = 2001$, with a residual sum of squares $= 3.379$ at the value $K = 0.65$. The analysis of variance can be set up to test the explanatory power of the

the analytical framework in which education's role is viewed is capable of handling nonneutral effects and indeed emphasizes their importance. The restrictive assumption of neutrality is imposed to simplify the framework sufficiently to permit empirical testing. These results seem to be broadly consistent with a positive effect of education on real full income—with an estimate of the elasticity of consumption income of around 0.65—but they also suggest that the simplification of nonneutrality is achieved at an appreciable cost.

It is interesting to compare these estimates of the elasticity of consumption income to the elasticity of money income with respect to education. To get an estimate of the market effect of education, using the same body of data, total consumption expenditure was regressed on education and the three other variables. The estimated constant elasticity of total consumption (and with the permanent income hypothesis, of money income as well) with respect to education, ϵ_{Y_mE}, was 0.793 (t value $= 10.87$). So the implied consumption-income elasticity of education is smaller than its market or money-income elasticity when the former is estimated by regression across items, and is of roughly equal magnitude when estimated by the iterative procedure just discussed.

In examining the direction and magnitude of education's effect on real full income through nonmarket efficiency, this study, instead of relying on any one test alone, has considered several measures. These—the qualitative item-by-item comparison, the two-way diagram or graph, the quantitative measures of the correlation between income and education elasticities, the slope coefficient, the value by iteration—all suggest that this effect is a positive one, although small in magnitude. The next two chapters present additional results which appear to be broadly consistent with this finding.

additional thirteen degrees of freedom that represent the thirteen nonneutral effects:

	Degree of Freedom	Sum of Squares	Mean Square	F
Nonneutrality	13	0.719	0.0553	41.34
Residual	1988	2.660	0.0013	
Constrained (total)	2001	3.379	0.0017	

Clearly the thirteen (net) additional parameters—the education elasticities—significantly reduce the residual variation. So this test suggests that education's effect is significantly nonneutral. It should be noted, however, that the manner in which K was estimated is not the most efficient test, since no effort was made to obtain and to use information on the covariation between residuals in the demand equations.

5

Detailed Expenditure Items

THE 1960 BLS consumer expenditure survey was also analyzed for more detailed expenditure items. The observations were again grouped by disposable income, education level of the head, and region as described in the previous chapter. The consumption items were disaggregated from the dozen or so used in Chapter 4 into fifty items (see Table 6), and two new items were added to the analysis—personal insurance expenditures and gifts and contributions. These are not included in the definition of total current consumption expenditure but are studied here as items that might also be interpreted via the model developed in the earlier chapters.

These fifty-two items vary considerably in size, from an average yearly expenditure of four dollars (on insurance for housefurnishings) to an average expenditure of nearly one thousand dollars (on food at home) per year. The relative variability in the expenditures also differs considerably among the items, from 33.7 per cent (on utilities) to 240.3 per cent (on real estate other than dwellings) of the mean. For the most part, the degree to which the items were disaggregated was dictated by the availability of the data (e.g., food at home was not available in any detail). However, some discretion was used in aggregating a few items (for instance, the "men's clothing" item is the sum of ten smaller items of outerwear, underwear, footwear, and so forth, for men of various age groups).

Naturally, many of these detailed expenditure items, as they are reported, have idiosyncrasies that raise various questions—say, about

TABLE 6
Detailed Expenditure Items

Item Number	Item	Mean Expenditure	Coefficient of Variation
	Total Current Consumption	5057	51.6
1.	Food at home	989	38.4
2.	Food away from home	245	66.9
3.	Alcohol	78	76.0
4.	Tobacco	91	39.3
5.	Rent expenditure	263	42.0
6.	Owned dwelling–interest on mortgages	119	91.7
7.	Owned dwelling–taxes	99	79.2
8.	Owned dwelling–insurance	27	73.5
9.	Owned dwelling–repairs	88	72.8
10.	Owned dwelling–other	17	134.6
11.	Owned vacation home	5	201.6
12.	Lodging out of town	35	139.3
13.	Other real estate	6	240.3
14.	Utilities	249	33.7
15.	Telephone	78	46.3
16.	Household services	105	115.1
17.	Household supplies	103	45.1
18.	Household textiles and floor coverings	59	75.9
19.	Household furniture	76	68.5
20.	Major appliances	69	54.1
21.	Small appliances	7	47.5
22.	Housewares	14	86.7
23.	Housefurnishings–insurance	4	112.3
24.	Housefurnishings–other	34	66.8
25.	Men's (age ≥ 18) clothing	137	69.6
26.	Women's clothing	192	72.4
27.	Clothing upkeep and materials	69	63.2
28.	Children's clothing	124	64.5
29.	Automobile purchase	301	74.3
30.	Automobile operations	396	54.6
31.	Public transportation	78	120.3
32.	Medical–prepaid (premiums)	89	44.0
33.	Medical–hospital	47	81.1
34.	Medical–outside hospital	55	46.1
35.	Medical–dental service	46	85.8
36.	Medical–eye care (including glasses)	16	56.8
37.	Medical–appliances, etc.	16	101.9
38.	Medical–drugs	69	36.2
39.	Personal care–services	65	56.2
40.	Personal care–supplies	80	40.9
41.	Television	38	42.9
42.	Radio, phonographs, etc.	33	87.4
43.	Spectator admissions	24	75.2
44.	Participation sports (equipment, fees)	30	93.4
45.	Club dues, hobbies, pets, toys, etc.	75	84.3
46.	Reading	44	58.6
47.	Education–tuition and fees	32	174.7
48.	Education–books, supplies	10	107.2
49.	Education–music and special lessons	11	189.7
50.	Miscellaneous personal consumption expenditure	111	100.6
51.	Personal insurance	315	79.0
52.	Gifts and contributions	280	96.9

the interpretation of their income elasticity. These make the observed expenditure a less than ideal measure of the service flow from these market goods used in nonmarket production. For example, the owned dwelling expenditure on interest payments on mortgages will necessarily be zero for all renters and all those homeowners who have no outstanding mortgage; or, the household expenditure on medical care prepaid premiums excludes employer-paid medical insurance. These and other similar instances seem to suggest that the expenditure items need some rather important adjustments before they can be analyzed and interpreted unambiguously.

This consideration would indeed be relevant if our interest were focused on a few specific items, or on each one in isolation. But since, instead, this study views the broad character of the expenditure pattern of households and, specifically, observes how this pattern changes in response to changes in certain economic and demographic characteristics of the household, it seems reasonable to take the items as they are—without much effort to adjust and "clean up" each one separately—and see whether the shifts in the expenditure pattern are systematic and predictable. Furthermore, while there is an abundant literature on the appropriate refinements one might make for accurately specifying the income-demand relationship for various items, attempts to adjust the large number of items analyzed here would be an expensive undertaking. So, both because of our principal interest centering on the aggregate shifts and our less than unlimited resources, no adjustment in any of the expenditure items was attempted at this time.

Two aspects of these detailed expenditure items do deserve attention. First, it has been repeatedly pointed out that, while education's effect has been assumed to be neutral (in the sense of affecting the productivity of all factors in all nonmarket production activities proportionately), it may not in fact be neutral, and if not, the empirical analysis should reveal the extent to which the neutrality model is an acceptable first approximation. The question arises, then: How would one expect the use of the more detailed expenditure items to affect the conformity of the empirical results with the neutrality model for any fixed degree of nonneutrality? In short, will the problem of the nonneutralities be exacerbated? Equation (1.18), which expresses the effect of the environmental variable, say education, on the demand for the market good, x_i, suggests that if education is biased toward or away from x_1, a change in the share w_{x1} has two effects.[1] These effects, through subsitution in consumption and substitution in production, work in opposite directions and their net effect is not at all evident. If the commodities are presumed to be the same for these more detailed items as for the more aggregated ones, then the greater detail means a lower w_{xi} for the item in question, and thus the effect of the greater disaggregation on $\tilde{x}_i$ (or ϵ_{iE}) is not a priori clear. That is, from this line of reasoning there appears to be no reason to anticipate greater difficulty from the nonneutrality with the more detailed classification of expenditures.

The second aspect of these more detailed items which deserves attention is the increased frequency of zero expenditures. While the procedure of using means from grouped data reduces the frequency of zeros considerably, the average expenditure on some narrowly defined items is frequently less than one dollar. Neither the zero expenditures nor the expenditures of a fraction of a dollar create any special problem in estimating linear or semilog functions,[2] but, when logarithms are used, the zeros cannot be manipulated and the high frequency of small positive expenditures increases the sensitivity to the manner in which the zeros are adjusted. Table 7 indicates the frequency of zero and fractional expenditures.

---

[1] Equation (1.18) can be written out as

$$\tilde{x}_i = \eta_i \tilde{Y}_e + \epsilon_i(\Pi_i/\Pi) - M\tilde{P}_{xi} + w_{ti}(\sigma + 1)(M\tilde{P}_{xi} - M\tilde{P}_{ti})$$

and, differentiating with respect to w_x,

$$\partial\tilde{x}_i/\partial w_{xi} = \epsilon_i[\partial(\Pi_i/\Pi)/\partial w_{xi}] - (\sigma + 1)(\tilde{MP}_{xi} - \tilde{MP}_{ti}).$$

The signs of these separate terms, when education is biased toward x_i, are

$$[(-)(-)] - [(+)(+)],$$

and if education is biased against x_i,

$$[(-)(+)] - [(+)(-)].$$

In neither case is the sign of the whole expression evident, nor would it be if the term $(\partial\sigma/\partial w_{xi})$ were nonzero.

[2] There is, of course, the problem of interpretation arising from the fact that in many instances zero expenditures are made by persons who are appreciably different from those who do spend—nonsmokers, homeowners, and families with no children spend nothing on tobacco, rent, and children's clothing, respectively.

TABLE 7
Number of Observations With Average Expenditure Under
One Dollar on an Expenditure Item

Item[a]	Number of Observations with an Expenditure of			Per Cent of Observations Spending Under One Dollar
	Zero	Fraction of One Dollar	Total	
11.	50	21	71	45.2
13.	30	27	57	36.3
10.	37	10	47	29.9
49.	23	15	38	24.2
23.	14	12	26	16.6
48.	8	15	23	14.6
47.	10	11	21	13.4
6.	15	3	18	11.5
21.	12	4	16	10.2
12.	10	4	14	8.9
28.	13	1	14	8.9
29.	14	0	14	8.9
44.	6	6	12	7.6
20.	11	1	12	7.6
37.	9	2	11	7.0
22.	7	3	10	6.4
41.	10	0	10	6.4
33.	8	1	9	5.7
5.	9	0	9	5.7
8.	7	1	8	5.1
19.	8	0	8	5.1
42.	4	4	8	5.1
7.	7	0	7	4.5
9.	7	0	7	4.5
18.	5	2	7	4.5
36.	6	1	7	4.5
3.	4	2	6	3.8
4.	6	0	6	3.8
43.	4	2	6	3.8
34.	5	0	5	3.2
35.	5	0	5	3.2
31.	4	0	4	2.5
25.	3	0	3	1.9

Note: All other items had two or less observations with zero expenditures and no observations with fractional expenditures.
[a] Items are defined in Table 6.

ELASTICITY ESTIMATES FOR DETAILED ITEMS

This section reports on the analysis of the Engel curves estimated for each of the fifty-two items where those observations that showed a zero expenditure were assigned an expenditure of one per cent per year.[3]

[3] This procedure differs from the one used in Chapter 4, which replaced the few existing zeros with a value of one dollar. The elasticities were also estimated for the detailed items using a one dollar figure where this was possible

For each of the fifty-two items listed in Table 6 several forms of the Engel curve were fitted. These were principally linear, semilog, constant elasticity, and constant elasticity with interaction (income-education and income-age) effects.[4] Since our main interest is in the relationship between income (consumption) elasticities and education elasticities, only those two coefficients will be presented in the tables that follow. Note, however, that in all cases the age of the head, the size of the family, and a South–non-South region dummy were also included linearly (unless their F ratio fell below the 0.005 level).

Table 8 presents the point estimates of the income elasticities, η_i, and the education elasticities, ϵ_{iE}, for fifty items obtained from weighted multiple regressions using the linear form. (The items are identified by numbers defined in Table 6). All these elasticities are computed at the mean values of the relevant variables.[5] The items "personal insurance" and "gifts" are not shown here in order to have a set of items that precisely exhausts the "total current consumption," C, and hence satisfies the constraint that the weighted income elasticity be unity (computationally, 0.9984) and the weighted average of the education elasticities be zero (computationally, -0.0016). Considering all fifty items in this linear form, we note that twenty-eight (56 per cent) of them, or 54 per cent of total consumption expenditure, exhibit the pre-

---

(i.e., where there were no fractional expenditures) and these are discussed later in this chapter.

Replacing the zeros with a small positive expenditure may appreciably affect the estimated coefficients compared to deleting the observations with zeros, especially where the frequency of zeros or small expenditures is high. (Such an item is "owned vacation homes," which has a mean of \$4.71 per year and on which 45 per cent of the observations spent less than one dollar per year.)

[4] The specific forms estimated for each item separately were

linear: $\qquad\qquad X_j = a + b_1 C_j + b_2 E_j + b_3 A_j + b_4 F_j + b_5 R_j + u_j$

semilog: $\qquad\quad X_j = a + b_1 \ln C_j + b_2 E_j + b_3 A_j + b_4 F_j + b_5 R_j + u_j$

double log (ln E): $\ln X_j = a + b_1 \ln C_j + b_2 \ln E_j + b_3 A_j + b_4 F_j + b_5 R_j + u_j$

double log (E): $\quad \ln X_j = a + b_1 \ln C_j + b_2 E_j + b_3 A_j + b_4 F_j + b_5 R_j + u_j$

interaction: $\qquad \ln X_j = a + b_1 \ln C_j + b_2 \ln E_j + b_3 A_j + b_4 F_j + b_5 R_j$
$$+ b_6 \ln C_j \ln E_j + b_7 \ln C_j \cdot A_j + u_j$$

where X_j = mean expenditure by the jth observation; C_j, E_j, A_j, F_j, and R_j are the observations' mean total consumption expenditure, mean level of education of the head, mean age of the head, mean family size, and region (South = 1; non-South = 0), for $j = 1, \ldots, 157$.

[5] For item 34, E was deleted since its F ratio was <0.005.

TABLE 8

Point Estimates of Income and Education Elasticities,
Linear Form[a]

Item[b]	Income Elasticity	Education Elasticity	Mean Expendi- ture	Item[b]	Income Elasticity	Education Elasticity	Mean Expendi- ture
1.	0.5280	−0.1397	989	26.	1.6595	−0.1101	192
2.	1.4450	−0.0211	245	27.	1.1867	0.1575	67
3.	1.4457	−0.3883	78	28.	0.6470	0.2448	124
4.	0.5280	−0.6007	91	29.	1.1319	−0.0883	301
5.	0.0423	−0.0367	263	30.	0.7832	−0.1584	396
6.	0.7710	1.1425	119	31.	2.3101	−0.3139	78
7.	1.3256	0.5345	99	32.	0.5613	0.1700	89
8.	1.4234	0.2619	27	33.	1.2272	−0.8504	47
9.	1.3356	−0.1718	88	34.	0.7302	0.0000	55
10.	1.4895	0.9734	17	35.	1.3490	0.6380	46
11.	3.3290	0.2347	5	36.	0.8245	0.0889	16
12.	3.1054	0.2701	35	37.	1.6251	−0.1877	16
13.	3.0082	0.3854	6	38.	0.5964	−0.1457	69
14.	0.4440	0.0838	249	39.	1.1412	−0.0189	65
15.	0.7978	0.2239	78	40.	0.5932	−0.1959	80
16.	2.6736	0.3680	105	41.	0.5424	−0.5069	38
17.	0.7553	0.0349	103	42.	1.1099	0.6516	33
18.	1.3106	0.1607	59	43.	1.5558	−0.0759	24
19.	1.0002	0.0637	76	44.	1.6696	0.1873	30
20.	0.6776	−0.1635	69	45.	1.5291	0.4945	75
21.	0.4074	−0.1925	7	46.	0.8328	0.6574	44
22.	1.6278	−0.7517	14	47.	3.0923	1.3583	32
23.	1.9035	0.1280	4	48.	0.7971	1.7852	10
24.	1.1619	0.2196	34	49.	3.2890	1.0242	11
25.	1.4643	−0.2263	137	50.	2.4964	−0.5013	111

[a] The estimates are computed at the point of means.
[b] Items defined in Table 6.

dicted qualitative relationship between η_i and ϵ_{iE}—no better than that which a random process might be expected to produce. Considering the magnitudes of the coefficients as well as their signs, the conformity is somewhat stronger, since the simple correlation between η_i and ϵ_{iE} is $+0.226$ (unweighted) and $+0.142$ (weighted by the expenditure shares). The quantitative estimate of the implied elasticity of consumption income will be presented below and discussed in comparison with estimates using other regression forms.

The Engel curves were also fitted using a semilog form, but in a vast majority of the cases the adjusted coefficient of determination was considerably lower than for the linear case, so this semilog form was not analyzed further. For seven of the fifty items the $\bar{R}^2$ was larger for the semilog form; their mean income and education elasticities, computed by the two methods, are compared in Table 9.

The Engel curves were also estimated assuming a constant income

TABLE 9
Semilog and Linear Elasticity Estimates

Item[a]	Semilog Form			Mean Expenditure	Linear Form		
	η_i	ϵ_{iE}	$\overline{R}^2$		η_i	ϵ_{iE}	$\overline{R}^2$
4.	0.6277	−0.4826	.828	91	0.5280	−0.6007	.815
5.	0.1911	−0.1321	.570	263	0.0423	−0.0367	.562
21.	0.5096	−0.1399	.544	7	0.4074	−0.1925	.530
32.	0.6350	0.3090	.887	89	0.5613	0.1700	.884
38.	0.6949	0.0000[b]	.748	69	0.5964	−0.1457	.731
40.	0.6750	−0.0427	.924	80	0.5932	−0.1959	.919
41.	0.6163	−0.3612	.653	38	0.5424	−0.5069	.650

[a] Items defined in Table 6.
[b] Variable dropped since its F ratio < 0.005.

elasticity, with the education variable entered linearly or logarithmically. Table 10 gives the resulting estimates of the two elasticities where the form with the higher adjusted-R^2 is used. In those cases in which $\overline{R}^2$ was higher with education entered linearly, the elasticity was com-

TABLE 10
Constant Elasticities

Item[b]	Income Elasticity	Education Elasticity	Mean Expenditure	Item[b]	Income Elasticity	Education Elasticity	Mean Expenditure
1.[a]	0.6403	−0.2008	989	27.	1.2373	0.0673	67
2.	1.2299	0.1789	245	28.[a]	0.4301	−0.3815	124
3.[a]	1.6663	−0.8131	78	29.[a]	1.7611	−1.2889	301
4.[a]	0.7382	−0.9225	91	30.[a]	1.1685	−0.4698	396
5.	−0.0863	−0.4588	263	31.[a]	1.6251	−0.1566	78
6.[a]	1.6531	−0.2048	119	32.[a]	0.8589	−0.0562	89
7.	1.0765	0.6964	99	33.[a]	0.5734	−0.6033	47
8.	0.9389	0.6272	27	34.	0.7809	−0.1850	55
9.	0.8999	0.0802	88	35.	1.4162	0.3858	46
10.[a]	0.9885	−0.2660	17	36.	0.7086	0.1295	16
11.[a]	3.2212	−0.8071	5	37.	0.7267	0.1874	16
12.	2.1942	0.3401	35	38.	0.6624	−0.1658	69
13.[a]	2.2491	−0.0944	6	39.	1.0754	0.0451	65
14.	0.4249	0.1527	249	40.[a]	0.7954	−0.3082	80
15.	0.9510	0.1476	78	41.[a]	0.8450	−0.9777	38
16.[a]	1.4495	0.7479	105	42.[a]	1.3338	0.0833	33
17.	0.8067	−0.0093	103	43.[a]	1.7705	−0.3453	24
18.[a]	1.0751	0.0171	59	44.[a]	1.7410	−0.1124	30
19.	1.2367	−0.6644	76	45.	1.5101	0.3089	75
20.[a]	0.5962	−0.4106	69	46.[a]	1.1362	0.3614	44
21.[a]	0.6591	−0.8362	7	47.[a]	2.3595	1.0350	32
22.[a]	1.1398	−0.4306	14	48.[a]	0.4970	1.2899	10
23.	0.8142	0.4782	4	49.	2.5946	0.5388	11
24.[a]	0.9328	0.2068	34	50.[a]	1.2415	0.1004	111
25.[a]	1.2694	−0.2600	137	51.[a]	1.3432	0.0934	315
26.	1.3958	0.0983	192	52.	1.7030	0.0970	281

[a] E is entered linearly; ϵ_{iE} at the mean E; $\overline{E} = 10.0384$.
[b] Items defined in Table 6.

puted at the mean level of education. For this set of estimates, qualitatively thirty-one of the items (60 per cent), or 68 per cent of total expenditure, were consistent with the predictions from the neutrality model.[6] While these results are stronger than in the linear case, quantitatively they are weaker when measured by the simple correlations between the elasticities: $+0.061$ (unweighted) or $+0.043$ (weighted).

Table 11 shows the elasticities computed at the means using the interaction form and forcing all the explanatory variables into the re-

TABLE 11
Point Estimates of Income and Education Elasticities,
Double-Log Form With Interaction Effects

Item[a]	Income Elasticity	Education Elasticity	Mean Expenditure	Item[a]	Income Elasticity	Education Elasticity	Mean Expenditure
1.	0.6239	−0.1814	989	27.	1.1902	0.1249	67
2.	1.2230	0.1933	245	28.	0.3293	−0.2889	124
3.	1.5754	−0.7554	78	29.	1.6323	−1.2168	301
4.	0.6001	−0.7875	91	30.	0.9928	−0.2279	396
5.	−0.0628	−0.4853	263	31.	1.3824	0.0685	78
6.	1.8253	−0.2788	119	32.	0.6879	0.1750	89
7.	1.3147	0.4575	99	33.	0.5177	−0.5642	47
8.	1.0645	0.5141	27	34.	0.8478	−0.2811	55
9.	0.8640	0.1323	88	35.	1.5288	0.2738	46
10.	2.0497	−1.2320	17	36.	0.6791	0.1669	16
11.	3.2974	−0.9445	5	37.	0.8082	0.0940	16
12.	1.9140	0.6357	35	38.	0.7505	−0.2669	69
13.	2.6497	−0.2550	6	39.	0.9399	0.1924	65
14.	0.4109	0.1660	249	40.	0.6786	−0.1390	80
15.	0.9655	0.1424	78	41.	0.6521	−0.7581	38
16.	1.4987	0.6074	105	42.	1.4126	−0.0245	33
17.	0.7934	0.0002	103	43.	1.4425	0.0626	24
18.	1.1084	−0.0514	59	44.	1.7642	−0.0473	30
19.	1.1006	−0.5709	76	45.	1.5874	0.2468	75
20.	0.7331	−0.5552	69	46.	1.1608	0.3561	44
21.	0.3144	−0.4857	7	47.	1.8122	1.4560	32
22.	1.0377	−0.3472	14	48.	0.4581	1.2284	10
23.	0.4948	0.7687	4	49.	2.5604	0.5999	11
24.	0.9617	0.1481	34	50.	1.4438	−0.2272	111
25.	1.2495	−0.2633	137	51.	1.3612	0.0106	315
26.	1.2486	0.2524	192	52.	1.6574	0.1413	281

[a] Items are defined in Table 6.

gression irrespective of their contribution to the total explanatory power of the equation. For this set of estimates twenty-eight (54 per cent) of the items, or 69 per cent of the total expenditure, were qualitatively consistent, while the correlations between η_i and ϵ_{iE} were again

---

[6] In this sense (with the sum of the expenditures used as weights) the total includes the two items "personal insurance" and "gifts." In no case, however, does the explanatory variable C include these items.

quite low and even negative in the unweighted case: -0.048 (unweighted) and $+0.080$ (weighted).

Since the interaction form was computed stepwise[7] and was permitted to delete any variable whose F ratio was below 0.005, a separate set of elasticity estimates is shown in Table 12, which uses that step with the highest $\bar{R}^2$.[8] With these estimates twenty-nine items (56

TABLE 12

Point Estimates of Income and Education Elasticities,
Double-Log Form With the Highest $\bar{R}^2$

Item[a]	Form[b]	Income Elasticity	Education Elasticity	Mean Expenditure	Item[a]	Form[b]	Income Elasticity	Education Elasticity	Mean Expenditure
1.	5	0.6420	−0.2008	989	27.	8	1.1869	0.1270	67
2.	5	1.2299	0.1789	245	28.	7	0.3293	−0.2889	124
3.	7	1.5754	−0.7554	78	29.	7	1.6323	−1.2168	301
4.	7	0.6001	−0.7875	91	30.	7	0.9928	−0.2279	396
5.	5	−0.0863	−0.4588	263	31.	7	1.3824	0.0685	78
6.	7	1.8253	−0.2788	119	32.	7	0.6879	0.1750	89
7.	7	1.3147	0.4575	99	33.	3	0.3236	−0.3926	47
8.	7	1.0645	0.5141	27	34.	8	0.8470	−0.2803	55
9.	4	0.9410	0.0687	88	35.	7	1.5288	0.2738	46
10.	7	2.0497	−1.2320	17	36.	5	0.7086	0.1295	16
11.	5	3.2482	−0.8381	5	37.	3	0.8618	0.1045	16
12.	8	1.9152	0.6340	35	38.	7	0.7505	−0.2669	69
13.	7	2.6497	−0.2550	6	39.	7	0.9399	0.1924	65
14.	5	0.4249	0.1527	249	40.	7	0.6786	−0.1390	80
15.	7	0.9655	0.1424	78	41.	7	0.6521	−0.7581	38
16.	7	1.4987	0.6074	105	42.	8	1.4123	−0.0260	33
17.	5	0.8067	−0.0093	103	43.	7	1.4425	0.0626	24
18.	6	1.1391	−0.0801	59	44.	7	1.7642	−0.0473	30
19.	7	1.1006	−0.5709	76	45.	7	1.5874	0.2468	75
20.	6	0.6485	−0.4808	69	46.	7	1.1608	0.3561	44
21.	7	0.3144	−0.4857	7	47.	7	1.8122	1.4560	32
22.	7	1.0377	−0.3472	14	48.	5	0.5644	1.1409	10
23.	7	0.4948	0.7687	4	49.	5	2.5946	0.5388	11
24.	6	0.9776	0.1349	34	50.	6	1.4577	−0.2399	111
25.	7	1.2495	−0.2633	137	51.	7	1.3612	0.0106	315
26.	7	1.2486	0.2524	192	52.	5	1.7030	0.0970	281

[a] Items are defined in Table 6.
[b] For the specific regression form, see footnotes 7 and 8.

[7] The order of entry of the explanatory variables was preassigned to be (1) $\ln C$, (2) $\ln E$, (3) A, (4) F, (5) R, (6) $(\ln C)(\ln E)$, (7) $(\ln C)A$.

[8] Here the linear estimates are not comparable (see p. 24) and were not considered. The second column in Table 12 indicates the step with the highest $\bar{R}^2$ where the last variable entered is seen from the previous footnote (i.e., a number 5 indicates the explanatory variables were $\ln C$, $\ln E$, A, F, R). For those items with a designation 8, some of the variables were forced out of the step since their F ratio <0.005. This occurred in four cases: in (12), $(\ln E)$ was dropped; in (27), (F) was dropped; in (34), (A) and $(\ln C)(A)$ were dropped; and in (42), (A) was dropped.

per cent), or 71 per cent of total expenditure, had the predicted sign, but again the correlation was small and even negative in the unweighted case: —0.006 (unweighted) and +0.096 (weighted).

Using each of the four sets of estimates of the income and education elasticities—from the linear, double-log, interaction, and highest $\overline{R}^2$ forms—the elasticity of consumption income was again estimated by regression. In addition to estimating this elasticity from equation (4.3), the regression was also run in the form

$$\epsilon_{iE} = a + b\eta_i + e_i, \tag{5.1}$$

since equation (4.3) is appropriate only when the weighted averages of the income and education elasticities are unity and zero, respectively. Table 13 summarizes these estimates of the elasticity of consumption income. These estimates (the slope coefficients b) vary considerably in the unweighted regressions, which give the same weight to each item regardless of the item's relative size in the consumption basket. The estimates in the weighted regressions, in three of the four cases, are quite similar, and also similar in magnitude to the estimate (0.084) from a weighted regression across the fifteen items discussed in the previous chapter. So, when estimated by weighted regression across the items in the consumption basket, the point estimate of the elasticity of consumption income is in the vicinity of 0.08, and, although not statistically significant, appears to be rather insensitive to the detail in which the consumption items are defined.

ELASTICITY ESTIMATES FOR COMPOSITE AND NONDURABLE ITEMS

This section reports on three modifications of the estimates given in the previous section: (1) replacing the zero values with an expenditure of one dollar per year; (2) grouping a few of the items into composites to reduce the frequency of extremely small or zero expenditures; and (3) estimating the elasticity of consumption income from a subset of nondurable items. The purpose of these few adjustments in the data was to obtain some further indication of the sensitivity of the estimates of ϵ_{Y_cE} to the treatment of the zeros and to the particular detail chosen for the expenditure items.

Replacing the zero expenditures by one dollar was possible only for those items that had no observations with positive average expenditures

TABLE 13

Summary of the Relationship Between Income and Education Elasticities Across Items

Set of Elasticity Estimates Used (Number of Items)	Means				Simple Correlation $(\epsilon_{iE}\eta_i)$		Regression Slope[a]		
	Weighted		Unweighted				$\epsilon_{iE} = a + b\eta_i$		$\epsilon_{iE} = b(\eta_i - 1)$
	ϵ_{iE}	η_i	ϵ_{iE}	η_i	Weighted	Unweighted	Weighted	Unweighted	Weighted
Linear Table 8 (50)	−0.0016	0.9984	0.1339	1.3456	0.142	0.226	0.0769 (1.00)	0.1415 (1.60)	0.0769 (1.01)
Constant Table 10 (52)	−0.1581	1.0463	−0.0564	1.1934	0.043	0.061	0.0372 (0.30)	0.0513 (0.43)	0.0077 (0.06)
Interaction Table 11 (52)	−0.1296	1.0145	−0.0388	1.1757	0.094	−0.030	0.0786 (0.66)	−0.0248 (−0.21)	0.0708 (0.58)
Highest $\bar{R}^2$ Table 12 (52)	−0.1349	1.0196	−0.0392	1.1777	0.096	−0.006	0.0788 (0.68)	−0.0053 (−0.05)	0.0679 (0.56)

[a] t values are in parentheses.

of less than one dollar. There were twenty-nine such items.[9] The point estimates of the elasticities, using the highest $\bar{R}^2$ from the stepwise regression, are shown in Table 14. A comparison of these elasticities with their counterparts in Table 12 reveals that for these items the coefficients are only very slightly affected by the treatment of the zeros, and in nearly all cases the same "step" gave the highest value for $\bar{R}^2$.[10] (The summary estimates were not computed due to their evident similarity to those in the earlier table.)

TABLE 14

Elasticity Estimates With Zeros Replaced by a
Yearly Expenditure of One Dollar

Item Number	η_i	ϵ_{iE}	Mean Expenditure	Item Number	η_i	ϵ_{iE}	Mean Expenditure
1.	0.6544	−0.2145	989	29.	1.7222	−1.0098	301
2.	1.2018	0.2242	245	30.	1.0023	−0.2413	396
4.	0.6065	−0.7213	91	31.	1.4010	0.0722	78
5.	0.1064	−0.3979	263	32.	0.7003	0.1579	89
7.	1.3462	0.4568	99	34.	0.8824	−0.2806	55
9.	0.9578	0.0680	88	35.	1.5697	0.2504	46
14.	0.4416	0.1316	249	38.	0.7551	−0.2762	69
15.	0.9698	0.1404	78	39.	0.9486	0.1842	65
16.	1.4853	0.6262	105	40.	0.6786	−0.1390	80
17.	0.8067	−0.0093	103	41.	0.6493	−0.6224	38
19.	1.0816	−0.4076	76	45.	1.5846	0.2694	75
24.	0.9910	0.1198	34	46.	1.1608	0.3561	44
25.	1.2522	−0.2520	137	51.	1.3703	−0.0051	315
26.	1.2612	0.2362	192	52.	1.7073	0.0895	281
27.	1.1869	0.1270	67				

Since the items with the most frequent zero expenditures were generally also those with frequent expenditures of a fraction of a dollar, the adjustment described in the previous paragraph was not made for them. Instead, a few of those items were combined into somewhat less detailed, homogeneous composite items which reduced the frequency of the zero and fraction expenditures. Table 15 indicates the items that were grouped and the resulting frequency of zeros and

[9] These may be identified from Table 7.

[10] There are four exceptions to this statement. In comparison with the results shown in Table 12, the four items had these changes in the highest $\bar{R}^2$ form when the zeros were replaced by one dollar (the numbers refer to the steps as defined in footnote 7, page 62): food away from home, step (6) instead of (8); automobile purchase, step (3) instead of (7); medical care–MD services, step (6) instead of (8); television, step (8) instead of (7), where (8) for television dropped the variable R.

TABLE 15
Definition of the Composite Items

Original Item	Item	Composite Item			
		Frequency of Zeros	Frequency of Fractions	Total	Per Cent of Observations Spending Less Than One Dollar
Owned dwelling Repairs Other	Owned dwelling miscellaneous	7	–	7	4.5
Owned vacation home Lodging out of town Other real estate	Other housing	8	2	10	6.4
Housefurnishings Insurance Other	Housefurnishings miscellaneous	1	–	1	0.6
Spectator admissions Participation sports	Sports	3	2	5	3.2
Education–tuition Education–books Education–lessons	Education	5	9	14	8.9

fractions in the five composite items. The Engel curves were estimated for each of these five, and the elasticities, evaluated at the means, are shown in Table 16 for the interaction and the highest $\bar{R}^2$ forms.

In comparison with the twelve detailed items, these composites are much more consistent with a positive effect of education on nonmarket productivity. Of the twelve, for the interaction form, only 33 per cent

TABLE 16
Elasticity Estimates, Composite Items

Composite Item	Mean Expenditures	Interaction Form			Highest $\bar{R}^2$ [a]		
		η_i	ϵ_{iE}	$\bar{R}^2$	η_i	ϵ_{iE}	$\bar{R}^2$
Owned dwelling miscellaneous	105	1.0030	0.1413	.638	0.9493	0.1967	.641
Other housing	46	2.0559	0.7313	.815	2.0427	0.6454	.816
Housefurnishings miscellaneous	39	0.9202	0.2568	.932	0.9202	0.2568	.932
Sports	54	1.5905	0.0774	.938	1.6047	0.0625	.939
Education	53	1.5374	1.3352	.843	1.5374	1.3352	.843

[a] *Form used in highest $\bar{R}^2$*:
Owned dwelling miscellaneous $\ln x_i = f (\ln C, \ln E, A, F)$
Other housing $\ln x_i = f (\ln C, \ln E, A, R, \ln C \cdot \ln E, \ln C \cdot A)$
Housefurnishings miscellaneous   Interaction form
Sports $\ln x_i = f (\ln C, \ln E, A, F, R, \ln C \cdot \ln E)$
Education   Interaction form

had the predicted sign; of the five composite items, 80 per cent had the correct sign.[11] Similarly, for the highest $\bar{R}^2$ the percentages of items conforming with the predicted signs rose from 33 per cent to 60 per cent. After substitution of these five items for their twelve sub-components in both the interaction and highest $\bar{R}^2$ forms, the qualitative relationship between η_i and ϵ_{iE} was reestimated. The resulting weighted and unweighted means, correlations, and regression slopes (unconstrained and forced through the origin) are presented in Table 18. For these sets of forty-five items the weighted correlations are higher than for the previous sets (about 0.14 compared to 0.09), and the regression slopes are somewhat higher (0.11 instead of 0.07) and somewhat less insignificant. The unweighted results were even more affected, and now show a positive correlation and statistically significant slope in all four cases.

Since the discussion in Appendix B suggests that biases in the estimates of the income and education elasticities are particularly strong in durable goods, the nondurables were selected from the fifty-two items, using the highest $\bar{R}^2$ form for the thirty-five nondurable items (or 81 percent of total expenditure). Table 17 lists the items considered to be nondurables.[12] Of these thirty-five items, twenty-six (74 per cent), or 84 per cent of the expenditure on nondurables, had the expected sign.[13]

---

[11] Even in the comparison of the weighted averages of the originally estimated elasticities there were significant improvements in the conformity with the model for "owned dwellings miscellaneous" and "other housing." The weighted averages for the interaction form computed from Table 11 are:

Item	η_i	ϵ_{iE}
Owned dwellings miscellaneous	1.0559	−0.0885
Other housing	2.1603	0.3477
Housefurnishings miscellaneous	0.9125	0.2134
Sports	1.6212	0.0015
Education	1.7119	1.2353

[12] The criterion used in selecting the "nondurables" was whether the expenditure made this year on some item would be likely to be made again in the following and subsequent years. Whether an expenditure is essentially a repetitive one or not was, in some cases, not intuitively clear, and the set of nondurables chosen here might have been a slightly different set.

[13] Of the seventeen durable items only three—major appliances, small appliances, and television sets—were consistent with the hypothesis.

TABLE 17
Nondurable Items

Item Number	Item	Item Number	Item
1.	Food at home	32.	Medical–prepaid (premiums)
2.	Food away from home	33.	Medical–hospital
3.	Alcohol	34.	Medical–outside hospital
4.	Tobacco	35.	Medical–dental service
5.	Rent expenditure	38.	Medical–drugs
7.	Owned dwelling–taxes	39.	Personal care–services
8.	Owned dwelling–insurance	40.	Personal care–supplies
12.	Lodging out of town	43.	Spectator admissions
14.	Utilities	44.	Participation sports
15.	Telephone		(equipment, fees)
16.	Household services	45.	Club dues, hobbies, pets,
17.	Household supplies		toys, etc.
23.	Housefurnishings–insurance	46.	Reading
25.	Men's (age ≥ 18) clothing	47.	Education–tuition and fees
26.	Women's clothing	48.	Education–books, supplies
27.	Clothing upkeep and materials	49.	Education–music and special
28.	Children's clothing		lessons
30.	Automobile operations	51.	Personal insurance
31.	Public transportation	52.	Gifts and contributions

The summary statistics, relating the two elasticities quantitatively and estimating b or ϵ_{Y_cE}, are given in Table 18. They show a relatively strong positive relationship—a weighted correlation of 0.53—and a statistically significant and relatively large regression slope of about 0.35.[14] This result suggests that the neutrality model is quite useful in interpreting the effect of education on the behavior of expenditures on these nondurable items.[15]

The iterative procedure discussed at the end of Chapter 4 was used again to obtain an estimate of the value of the consumption income

[14] This slope coefficient is smaller than that obtained from a nondurable subset reported in Table C.8, but the two sets are not really comparable since the latter one used nondurables taken from the less detailed set of items and presumably represented the nondurables less adequately.

Also, the set reported here did not use any of the composite items that probably would have further increased the positive relationship between the elasticity estimates. Since the composites were not used, the results shown for nondurables are most directly comparable to those for the set of highest $\overline{R}^2$ items in Table 12.

[15] The nondurables were also run for the set of constant elasticity estimates taken from Table 10. The results for the weighted regression were $b = 0.2834$ (2.51) with a correlation of 0.401, and, when forced through the origin, $b = 0.2881$ (2.52). The unweighted regression slope b was 0.2404 (1.71) with a correlation of 0.285. Thus, these nondurable estimates also show a strong positive relationship and a sizable elasticity of consumption income.

TABLE 18

Summary of the Relationship Between Income and Education Elasticities Across Items Composites and Nondurables

Set of Elasticity Estimates Used (Number of Items)	Means				Simple Correlation $(\epsilon_{iE}\eta_i)$		Regression Slope[a]		
	Weighted		Unweighted				$\epsilon_{iE} = a + b\eta_i$		$\epsilon_{iE} = b(\eta_i - 1)$
	ϵ_{iE}	η_i	ϵ_{iE}	η_i	Weighted	Unweighted	Weighted	Unweighted	Weighted
Interaction with composites (45)	−0.1202	1.0108	−0.0451	1.0663	0.141	0.342	0.1224 (0.93)	0.3457 (2.39)	0.1166 (0.86)
Highest $\bar{R}^2$ with composites (45)	−0.1232	1.0135	−0.0416	1.0633	0.136	0.336	0.1160 (0.90)	0.3283 (2.34)	0.1087 (0.82)
Highest $\bar{R}^2$ nondurables only (35)	−0.0439	0.9476	0.1239	1.1023	0.530	0.363	0.3509 (3.59)	0.3103 (2.24)	0.3566 (3.71)

[a] t values are in parentheses.

elasticity. Imposing the neutrality constraint for various values of K, equation (4.5) was estimated for each of the forty-five items that included the five "composites" and for each of the thirty-five non-durable items. Table 19 indicates the overall weighted residual sums of squares for given values of K in both cases. That value of K which minimizes this residual is similar in magnitude to the value indicated in Table 5 that utilized the set of fourteen broader expenditure categories. This iterative procedure suggests that the value of K, the esti-

TABLE 19

Overall Residual Sums of Squares of the Detailed Items,
by Values of the Elasticity of Consumption Income K

| Value of K | Weighted Residual Sum of Squares | | Value of K | Weighted Residual Sum of Squares | |
	45 *Composites*	*35* *Nondurables*		*45* *Composites*	*35* *Nondurables*
−1.00	16.198	11.938	0.50	13.470	9.643
0.00	13.765	9.822	0.75	13.447	9.651
0.10	13.663	9.751	1.00	13.457	9.682
0.30	13.533	9.670	2.00	13.585	9.847
0.40	13.495	9.651	5.00	13.860	10.133

mate of the elasticity of consumption income, is in the range of 0.50 to 0.75. The detail in which the items are defined—fourteen broad items or forty-five more narrowly defined items—appears to have very little influence on the estimated magnitude of K. The estimate of this elasticity from the iterative procedure is significantly higher than the estimate obtained from the weighted regression across the independent items.[16] This was also the case in the previous chapter.

While these various point estimates of the effect of education on real full income through nonmarket efficiency—the consumption in-come elasticity—vary in magnitude with the different techniques of estimation, they appear to be broadly consistent with a positive effect. The estimates from a weighted regression across all items suggest a

---

[16] Employing the method discussed in footnote 22 of Chapter 4, the value of F is 152.15 for the forty-five composites, with an estimate of $K = 0.75$. Similarly, the F value is 92.89 for the thirty-five nondurables, with an estimate of $K = 0.50$. In both cases the value of K with the lowest residual variation shows a significant improvement over a value of zero.

If the standard errors of K are again estimated from these F values (see footnote 22, Chapter 4), they are $\hat{\sigma} = 0.061$ for the forty-five items, and $\hat{\sigma} = 0.052$ for the thirty-five nondurables.

very low magnitude which is not statistically significant. But when only nondurable goods are considered, the magnitude of this elasticity is about 0.35 and statistically different from zero. By contrast, the iterative procedure imposes neutrality with various values of the consumption income elasticity, and the value that minimizes the residual variation is in the range of 0.50 to 0.75. While these point estimates differ appreciably from one estimation technique to another, there is a tendency for the regression across items to imply a smaller value than that implied by the iterative procedure, while the detail in which the expenditure items are defined appears to have very little influence on the estimates. The following chapter briefly discusses additional evidence from other data sources.

6

Additional Empirical Evidence

THREE APPLICATIONS of the model are made in this chapter. The first utilizes a portion of the Bureau of Labor Statistics' 1950 survey of consumer expenditures, which is quite similar in nature to the 1960–61 survey used in the previous chapters. The second is a reexamination of some previously published evidence on consumption patterns in Israel. The environmental variable approach discussed above is used to interpret a pattern of behavior that was previously ascribed to differences in tastes. The third application is a very brief investigation of the demand for children. In all three, the approach developed in the earlier chapters offers a generally consistent interpretation of the observed effect of education on consumption patterns.

1950 BLS CONSUMER EXPENDITURES SURVEY

The Bureau of Labor Statistics' *Study of Consumer Expenditures, Incomes and Savings, 1950,* covering 12,489 consumer units, is similar in design and nature to the 1960 survey analyzed in the previous two chapters. In the 1950 survey the household data are published in cross-classified tables in which the mean expenditures and mean values of various household characteristics are given. One important difference from the 1960 survey is that the published form of the 1950 data is more extensively cross-classified. The empirical investigation discussed in this section is limited to the North region data, containing approximately 45 per cent of the households surveyed. These 5,724 households are cross-classified by disposable income (nine groups), education (four groups), and city size (three groups) into 103 observations (five null cells).[1]

The average cell for these data contained slightly more than fifty households, compared to an average cell size of approximately eighty-seven households in the 1960 data. Recalling that the primary reason for using the grouped data from these surveys is to reduce the biases resulting from measurement error in the income variable, note that the more detailed cross-classification, which lowers the cell size, presumably reduces this bias less adequately. Also, with the more disaggregated data, we can generally expect smaller coefficients of determination, ceteris paribus, according to Cramer.[2]

The expenditures were again first grouped into goods and services. The goods component includes expenditures for food at home, alcohol, tobacco, housing (defined as rent paid by renters, as in the 1960 data),[3] utilities, housefurnishings, clothing, reading, and automobile purchases. The service component includes food away from home, household operations, personal care, medical care, recreation, education, automobile operations, and travel expenses other than automobile. These two items were regressed on total consumption expenditures, C, the education of the head of the family, E, the age of the head, A, and the household size, F, in the same manner as for the 1960 survey. The elasticity estimates are shown in Table 20.

TABLE 20

Elasticity Estimates for Goods and Services, 1950 BLS Data, North Region

Item	Income Elasticity	Education Elasticity	Family Size Elasticity	$\bar{R}^2$
Linear[a]				
Goods	0.934	−0.051	0.058	.991
Services	1.397	0.064	−0.472	.983
Constant elasticity				
Goods	0.909	−0.019	0.122	.994
Services	1.305	0.070	−0.382	.989

[a] The elasticities are evaluated at the means of the relevant variables.

[1] Even more narrowly defined cells—adding an occupational breakdown of seven categories—were available. These, too, were investigated, and Appendix D discusses some of the results.

[2] J. S. Cramer, "Efficient Grouping, Regression, and Correlation in Engel Curve Analysis," *Journal of the American Statistical Association,* March 1964.

[3] Since this housing variable is not defined for cells without renters, the goods component here had ninety-six observations, i.e., seven of the 103 cells had no renters. The service component does include all 103 observations.

These results are roughly the same as the corresponding ones for the 1960 data. In comparing these two sets of results, it must be kept in mind that the discussion in Chapter 4 holds the region constant by means of a South–non-South dummy, while the data here apply exclusively to the North region. As in the previous chapter, the goods component has an income elasticity of less than unity, while services are a luxury. The education effect in these two cases suggests that an increase in education consistently shifts expenditures toward the luxury, with an increase in family size shifting expenditures toward the necessity. It should be stressed, when interpreting these results, that the restriction on the weighted mean value of the education and family-size coefficients leaves only one degree of freedom for each coefficient in the two regressions.[4]

For these data, too, the Engel curve was estimated separately for each of the expenditure items. Here the zero values for expenditures were replaced by a value of one; the number of zeros for the items are shown in the table below.

Item	Number of Zero Values for Each Item
Education	10
Automobiles (purchases)	8
(Rent)[a]	(7)
Alcohol	2
Tobacco	2
All other	0

[a] Since the rental item had a zero value only where the percentage of renters in the cell was also zero, these observations were deleted (see footnote 3).

Table 21 presents the estimated income, education, and family-size elasticities for each item using the form which gave the highest adjusted $-R^2$. It is tempting to make a detailed comparison of these elasticities with those in Table 4. Readers making such a comparison should keep in mind that the 1960 data include all regions while the 1950 data include only the North. Notice, in particular, that housing and housefurnishings are luxuries in the 1950 data, that the education effects for clothing and leisure have reversed their sign, and that the travel expenditures are not comparable since automobile operations expenditures are included in "automobile" for 1960 and in "travel (service)" for 1950.

[4] Obviously, the constraint is not precisely satisfied in this case, since the two sets of point estimates contain different numbers of observations (see footnote 3).

For the fifteen items in Table 21, food at home, tobacco, and personal care are necessities with negative education effects; food away, housing, household operations, education, and the two travel expenditure items are luxuries with positive education effects. The remaining six items cannot be consistently interpreted within the context of the neutrality model for education. Alcohol, utilities, and medical care were similarly "nonneutral" in the 1960 data. The additional three items are housefurnishings, clothing, and leisure. One possible explanation for the results for housefurnishings and clothing lies in the durables bias discussed in Appendix B. If the smaller cell size of the 1950 data increases the durables bias, it could explain why the income elasticities are appreciably higher (and the education coefficients lower) in the 1950 estimates.

TABLE 21

Elasticity Estimates, 1950 BLS Data, North Region,

Form with Highest $\bar{R}^2$

Item	Income Elasticity	Education Elasticity	Family Size Elasticity	$\bar{R}^2$	Mean Expenditure	Form
Food (home)	0.4328	−0.1179	0.6833	.9803	978	7
Food (away)	1.8361	0.0990	−1.5458	.8824	224	2[a]
Alcohol	1.3317	−0.5261	−0.2101	.8615	75	2[a]
Tobacco	0.7189	−0.6298	0.0944	.8931	72	4
Housing	1.2179	0.2273	−0.6465	.9030	553	7
Utilities	0.0514	0.4648	1.2426	.7765	171	7
Household operations	1.2807	0.3493	−0.6205	.9562	187	7
Housefurnishings	1.3450	−0.2416	0.0390	.9194	259	7
Clothing	1.4041	−0.0857	−0.2132	.9880	465	5[b]
Personal care	0.9123	−0.1228	−0.1231	.9769	88	5
Medical care	0.8688	0.1381	0.1760	.8724	201	7
Leisure	1.3987	−0.1995	−0.0131	.9688	218	7
Education	2.5419	1.2538	−0.3991	.7936	25	7
Auto (purchases)	1.1685	0.1285	0.5251	.8018	237	2[a]
Travel (service)	1.0299	0.0496	0.4473	.9615	256	5

Note: Regression forms are as follows:

1: $X_i = f\ (C, E, A, F)$
2: $X_i = f\ (C, E, A, A^2, F)$
3: $\ln X_i = f\ (\ln C, \ln E, A, \ln F)$
4: $\ln X_i = f\ (\ln C, \ln E, A, A^2, \ln F)$
5: $\ln X_i = f\ (\ln C, \ln E, A, F, (\ln C \cdot \ln E), (\ln C \cdot A))$
6: $\ln X_i = f\ (\ln C, \ln E, \ln A, \ln F)$
7: $\ln X_i = f\ (\ln C, \ln E, A, \ln F, (\ln C \cdot \ln E),$
$(\ln C \cdot A), (\ln C \cdot \ln F))$

[a] In the three cases in which the dependent variable is linear, the adjusted $-R^2$ is considerably higher than in the best logarithmic form: food (away): 0.8824 (linear), 0.8447 (form 7); alcohol: 0.8615 (linear), 0.7843 (form 7); auto purchases: 0.8018 (linear), 0.7022 (form 5). In all other cases the logarithmic form gave the highest $\bar{R}^2$, but see footnote 3, Chapter 3.

[b] Uses $(\ln F)$ instead of (F).

To obtain a quantitative measure of the relationship between the income and education elasticities and of the implied elasticity of consumption income, regressions were run across Engel curves in the manner already discussed in the preceding chapters. The observations are the estimates for each item shown in Table 21; the regression was run once weighted by expenditure shares and forcing the intercept to be zero, and again in weighted and unweighted form without forcing the regression line through the origin. Table 22 indicates that in each case the slope coefficient—the estimate of the consumption-income elasticity—is positive, although not statistically significant. The point

TABLE 22

Summary of the Relationship Between Income and Education
Elasticities Across Items, 1950 BLS, North Region

| Weighting Procedure | Means | | Correlation $(\epsilon_{iE}\eta_i)$ | Regression[a] | | $\epsilon_{iE} = b(\eta_i - 1)$ |
| | ϵ_{iE} | η_i | | $\epsilon_{iE} = a + b\eta_i$ | | |
				a	b	b
Weighted by expenditure shares	0.009	1.016	0.082	−0.047	0.055	0.056
				(−0.30)	(0.40)	(0.40)
Unweighted	0.052	1.169	0.410	−0.317	0.316	0.315
				(−1.25)	(1.62)	(1.75)

[a] t values are in parentheses.

estimate here, $+0.05$, is smaller than the estimates derived from the 1960 BLS data, as summarized in Table 18 for the forty-five categories of total expenditure $(+0.11)$ or as summarized in Table 13 for the fifty-two detailed categories $(+0.08)$.

Considering all the estimates of the slope coefficient from weighted regressions across items from Chapters 4, 5, and 6, as well as Appendix C, the value appears to be in the general vicinity of one-tenth when all items are included.[5] In this general sense the evidence from the 1950 BLS survey for the North region tends to support the conclusion drawn from the 1960 survey that the consumption-income elasticity is positive, although relatively small in magnitude.

Total consumption expenditure from the 1950 data was regressed as before on the other three independent variables to obtain an estimate of the elasticity of total consumption (or money income) with

[5] The subset of nondurables discussed in the previous chapter and in Appendix C consistently yields a higher estimate of the elasticity. The unweighted estimates for the whole group are not as easily summarized since they are considerably more erratic.

respect to education. The estimate of this elasticity, in double-log form, was 0.817 ($t = 10.79$), which is also quite similar to the estimate from the 1960 data of 0.793 (see Chapter 4). So the evidence from the earlier survey broadly supports the conclusions reached on the basis of the more recent BLS data in the last two chapters: in the context of the analytical framework suggested here, education appears to have a small positive effect on real full income, an effect which is smaller than the implied money-income elasticity of education when estimated by a single regression across expenditure elasticities.

CONSUMPTION PATTERNS IN ISRAEL

Reexamining the findings of two studies of consumption patterns in Israel within the theoretical framework developed in this study has yielded some interesting results. The first, by Liviatan, is based on a family expenditures survey of 6,500 Jewish wage-earning families living in cities of over 10,000 for the period May 1956–May 1957, with each month representing an independent sample of new families.[6] The unique feature of these data is that 5,800 of the families surveyed were immigrants, that is, the head of the family was not born in Israel.

Liviatan studied the consumption patterns separately for Euro-American (E) immigrants (4,211 families) and Afro-Asian (A) immigrants (1,581 families). For each of the two groups he estimated the equation

$$X = b_0 + b_1 C + b_2 \log S, \tag{6.1}$$

where X is the expenditure on the good, C is total consumption, and S is family size. The regression also held constant the duration of residence and occupation, given the assumption that these variables affect only the level and not the slope of the consumption functions.[7] The estimated income elasticities, computed at the overall sample means, are given in Table 23 below.

[6] Nissan Liviatan, *Consumption Patterns in Israel*, Jerusalem, Falk Project for Economic Research in Israel, 1964.

[7] The data were grouped by duration of residence and by occupation and the variables X, C, and S were expressed as deviations from their mean within the cells from the two-way classification. The effects of these two additional variables can be analyzed by adjusted means, discussed below. Also, for the regressions for nonfood expenditures, disposable income, Y, and family size, S, were used as instrumental variables since the data were not grouped by Y. For food expenditures, the log of C was used; see Liviatan, Chapters 4 and 5 for the details of the estimation procedure.

TABLE 23

Income Elasticities and Relative Levels of Consumption in Israel by Continent of Origin and Duration of Residence

| Item | Income Elasticity | | E − A | EN − AN | EV − AV | AV − AN | EV − EN |
	Asian (1)	European (2)	A (Per Cent) (3)	AN (Per Cent) (4)	AV (Per Cent) (5)	AN (Per Cent) (6)	EN (Per Cent) (7)
Clothing	1.527	1.420	−27.5	−28.8	−21.2	−12.0	−2.6
Footwear	1.204	0.465	−15.8	−14.0	−10.0	−14.5	−10.5
Durables	1.505	2.313	−10.4	−7.7	−17.6	+12.8	+0.7
House maintenance	0.765	0.784	+16.7	+12.4	+14.3	+10.1	+11.9
Tobacco	0.482	0.776	−25.7	−16.2	−32.0	−3.6	−21.9
Education	2.001	1.216	+136.9	+92.3	+124.4	+29.3	+50.8
Literary	1.858	1.710	+93.4	+74.9	+99.6	+9.0	+24.4
Health	1.303	1.276	+70.0	+70.8	+31.4	+50.8	+16.0
Fees	1.403	1.240	+21.3	+25.6	+20.8	+4.5	−8.2
Entertainment	1.814	2.145	−4.7	+5.0	−21.6	+29.1	−3.5
Total food	0.582	0.516	−2.0	−0.3	−3.6	+0.5	−2.8

Source: N. Liviatan, *Consumption Patterns in Israel*, pp. 50–69.

The aspect of this Israeli study of particular interest in the context of the model developed here is that the continent of origin as well as the duration of stay in Israel are shown to have an effect on consumption patterns. Liviatan investigated the consumption level of various goods and related the differences in these levels to the continent of origin. From the fact that consumption patterns were found to differ between the two groups E and A after differences due to income and family size had been removed, Liviatan concluded, "We may therefore ascribe the remaining differences largely to differences in taste."

But since we can ascertain the relative educational attainment of the various continent groups, we may interpret their different consumption patterns as resulting from variations in the amounts of their human capital.[8] These educational differences are suggested by another Falk Institute publication, which states: "Continent of origin and length of residence in Israel are also connected with level of education: persons of European origin are concentrated in higher levels of education than persons from Asia and Africa, and the level of education rises together with the duration of residence in the country."[9] More specifically, Appendix E estimates the educational attainment of the four groups—European veterans (EV), European new immigrants (EN), Afro-Asian veterans (AV), and Afro-Asian immigrants (AN)—and indicates that the education level rises monotonically from (AN) to (AV) to (EN) to (EV), for males and females separately. Consequently, we can expect to observe that the more educated European veterans consume relatively more of the luxuries and less of the necessities (after removing the effects of money income and family size)—relative, that is, to the other groups. Similarly, the veteran Asians, AV, would be expected to shift their consumption pattern toward luxuries vis-à-vis the new immigrants from Asia, AN.

To test this, we may use Liviatan's study of differences in consumption levels by continent and duration of residence. This is done by an analysis of adjusted means. The adjusted mean, or calculated consumption level, is

$$X_j{}^* = \overline{X}_j + b_{1j}(\overline{C} - \overline{C}_j) + b_{2j} (\overline{\log S} - \overline{\log S_j}), \qquad (6.2)$$

[8] We compare the groups only with respect to years of formal schooling, but the continent of origin may reflect a more general human capital variable, including health and other forms.

[9] Ruth Klinov-Malul, *The Profitability of Investment in Education in Israel*, Jerusalem, Falk Project for Economic Research in Israel, 1966, p. 5.

where j is an index of continent of origin and duration of residence; $\overline{X}_j$, $\overline{C}_j$, and $\overline{\log S}_j$ are the average consumption of good X, total consumption, and log of family size in each group; and $\overline{C}$ and $\overline{\log S}$ are the overall sample means. The comparison of levels between groups does "not take into account the differences between the continents in occupational [or educational] structure and distribution by duration of residence. . . . [The] comparison therefore shows the differences between families of Asian and European immigrants who have the same incomes and family size but retain the occupational structure and distribution by duration of residence of their continent group as a whole."[10]

Columns 3–7 of Table 23 compare the levels of consumption for the eleven subcomponents of total expenditure by continent of origin (columns 3–5) and duration of residence (columns 6 and 7), expressing differences as a percentage of the less educated group's consumption level.[11] In column 3, for example, which covers families irrespective of duration of residence, a positive figure implies that the Europeans spent more on the good, with income and family size held constant. Our model leads us to expect positive values for goods with income elasticities greater than unity and negative values for goods with income elasticities less than unity. The same predicted signs hold for all columns, since all are defined in the same way—relative to the less educated group.

To determine how well this predicted relationship holds, we may use the two-way schematic diagram as before, without, however, referring to statistical significance. For the $(E - A)/A$ comparison in column 3 we have:

Human Capital		*Income Elasticity*
	$\eta > 1$	$\eta < 1$
(+)	Education Literary Health Fees	House mainte- nance
(−)	Clothing Durables Entertainment	Tobacco Food

[10] Liviatan, *Consumption Patterns in Israel*, p. 64.

[11] For example, the $X_A{}^*$ for clothing is 33.68 and the $X_B{}^*$ is 24.42. That is, given the same income and family size (the overall mean income and S), the

In this instance the predictions held in six out of ten cases (footwear cannot be judged in intercontinent comparisons since its estimated income elasticity changes from 0.46 to 1.20 between continents). In each of the other four comparisons the predictions were at least as good: (EV − AV)/AV (column 5), 6 out of 10; (EN − AN)/AN (column 4), 7 out of 10; (EV − EN)/EN (column 7), 7 out of 11; and (AV − AN)/AN (column 6), 7 out 11. In all cases at least 60 per cent of the items were consistent with the model.

Of even more importance is the stability seen here, both internally and in comparison with the U.S. data. Seven of these items showed the same sign for each comparison; thus the ranking for, say, "literary" was: AN spent less than AV who spent less than EN who spent less than EV, which is as expected, given the education ranking of the four groups. Also, at least six of the items for these Israeli data are in the same "cell" as in the BLS data, and only one is consistently in another cell (health consumption, as defined here, is a luxury).

Our interpretation of these expenditure patterns goes far in resolving what was a puzzle to Liviatan. He states:

> The 'continent effect' works in the same direction both for new-comers and veterans . . . [and] . . . there is no general tendency for the differences between continents to be reduced (i.e., to be smaller for veterans). . . . While the effect of duration of residence on Asian immigrants lends itself to a simple interpretation—mainly, as a desire to imitate the European standards—it is difficult to rationalize the effect of duration of residence on *European* immigrants.[12]

He also indicates:

> For reasons we were not able to determine, the European immigrants tend to change their nonfood consumption patterns in precisely the same direction as the Asian immigrants.[13]

Our interpretation does not suggest that Asian veterans try to imitate Europeans or change their tastes toward European patterns. Rather,

Asian household (using *its* estimated coefficients) would spend 33.68 IL [Israeli pound] per month on clothing, etc. Then

$$(E − A)/A = (24.42 − 33.68)/33.68 = − 9.26/33.68 = − 0.275.$$

Given the same (mean) income and family size, the European household would spend 27 per cent less on clothing. Similarly, (EV − AV)/AV is the computed level of the European veterans' consumption relative to the computed level of the Asian veterans' consumption.

[12] Liviatan, *Consumption Patterns in Israel*, p. 67.

[13] Ibid., p. 10.

we suggest that they have more human capital than Asian newcomers, are consequently more productive in consumption, and thus have—and behave as if they had—more real income. Similarly, our interpretation of the European newcomers vis-à-vis European veterans is that the latter possess more human capital than the former, and thus have a higher real income through increased consumption income.

This same pattern exists when Liviatan briefly compares the behavior of "clerks" (nonmanual workers) with that of "laborers" (manual workers). He finds the clerks' educational level to be considerably higher than that of laborers and writes:

> The effect of occupation on nonfood expenditures tends to be in the same direction as the effect of continent. In particular, the pattern of differences between European and Asian immigrants is of the same type as the differences between clerks and laborers within each immigrant group. This suggests that the differences in nonfood consumption patterns between continents is primarily the result, not of the particular 'traditions' of the two continents as such, but of more general factors, such as formal education.[14]

In sum, in all of these comparisons between continents of origin, duration of stay, and occupation, the model developed in this study has proved useful in interpreting the observed patterns of consumption.

A similar study was made by Paroush based on the Israeli family expenditure survey for 1963–64, a more recent survey comparable in design and character to the one used by Liviatan.[15] Paroush also estimates income elasticities and family-size elasticities for the various components of total consumption, and compares the levels of consumption for the two continents of origin, E and A, by using the analysis of adjusted means. His relevant results are shown in Table 24.

With these data our two-way diagram shows:

Human Capital	*Income Elasticity*	
	$\eta > 1$	$\eta < 1$
(+)	Durables Culture	House maintenance Health
(−)	Clothing	Food Fruits Vegetables Footwear Tobacco

[14] Ibid., p. 71.

[15] Jacob Paroush, "Hefreshay Tzrechan Bain Schechavoth Ha-ochlusiah" ["Differences in Consumption Between Various Strata of the Population"],

TABLE 24

Income Elasticities in Israel by Continent of Origin, 1963–64 Survey

Consumption Item	Income Elasticity A	E	Adjusted Means (E − A)
Total food (excluding fruits and vegetables)	0.500	0.403	−6.29
Clothing	1.465	1.015	−6.97
Footwear	0.734	0.663	−1.10
Durables	1.079	1.173	+10.10
House maintenance	0.573	0.762	+7.73
Tobacco	0.478	0.494	−3.20
Education	1.322	0.941	+15.32
Culture	1.383	1.225	+4.29
Health	0.652	0.864	+8.11
Fruits	0.807	0.525	−0.62
Vegetables	0.379	0.369	−2.04

Source: See footnote 15.

Seven of the ten items are consistent with the prediction from the neutrality model (eight of eleven items if we include education as a luxury, which has been the case consistently elsewhere). Thus, the results for these data are also consistent with the predicted behavior in at least 70 per cent of the cases, and the configuration of the items in the two Israeli studies is quite similar. In explaining these gross comparisons of expenditure patterns by continent of origin, our model offers a fairly consistent interpretation and is a viable alternative to an explanation based on differences in taste.

CHILDREN AS A CONSUMPTION ITEM

Throughout this paper the family-size coefficients have been given several alternative interpretations—one based on complementarity, one based on production efficiency, and one based on externalities of scale. A discussion of the determinants of the family size itself is considered beyond the scope of this project, so the F variable has been taken as an exogenous one for the Engel curve analysis. If, however, the decision to have children *is* a conscious consumption decision on the part of the family, then the same reasoning applies to the consumption good "children" as to any other item in the commodity basket—if the income elasticity of children is less than unity, the effect of educa-

Riv'on Le Chalchlah [*Economic Quarterly*], June 1966. I am indebted to Jacob Paroush for bringing this study to my attention.

tion would be negative, given the positive value of ϵ_{Y_cE} and assuming "neutrality."

Using the 1960 BLS data, cross-classified in the same way as in Chapter 4, the average number of children under the age of eighteen was regressed on total consumption, education of head, age of head, region, and the percentage of nonwhites. The results are shown in Table 25. The linear regressions had 157 observations; the logarithmic regressions contained 142 observations, since they exclude those cells

TABLE 25

Elasticity Estimates on the Demand for Children, 1960 BLS Data

A. Simple Correlation Matrix

	Education	Age	Family Size	Per Cent Nonwhite	Region	Children
Consumption	0.536	−0.516	0.727	−0.633	−0.197	0.592
Education		−0.693	0.210	−0.599	−0.191	0.343
Age			−0.633	0.465	0.035	−0.772
Family size				−0.317	0.074	0.921
Per cent nonwhite					0.540	−0.308
Region						0.062

B. Regression on Number of Children

	ln C	E_1[a]	E_2	E_3	Age	Per Cent Non-white	Region
Children	0.6346	−0.4121	−0.1551	−0.0722	−0.0634	2.3707	0.0359
t values	(8.70)	(−5.41)	(−2.30)	(−0.56)	(−11.96)	(5.50)	(0.59)
Partial correlation	0.60	−0.42	−0.19	−0.05	−0.72	0.43	0.05

C. Mean Elasticities, Various Regression Forms

Form[b]	Income Elasticity	Education Elasticity	Age Elasticity	Implied Consumption Income Elasticity
1.	0.344	−0.537	−2.113	0.819
2.	0.347	−0.538	−2.094	0.824
3.	0.499	−0.943	−3.231	1.882
4.	0.340	−0.853	−3.098	1.292
5.	0.496	−0.763	−3.049	1.514

[a] E_1, E_2, E_3 are education dummies for high school, college, postgraduate; see Appendix C.

[b] Definition of form:

		Number of observations	$\bar{R}^2$
1: $x = f(C, E, A, NW, R)$		157	.769
2: $x = f(C, E, A, NW, R)$		142	.761
3: $\ln x = f(\ln C, \ln E, A, R)$		142	.808
4: $\ln x = f(\ln C, \ln E, A, R, (\ln C \cdot \ln E), (\ln C \cdot A))$		142	.836
5: $\ln x = f(\ln C, \ln E, A, NW, R, (\ln C \cdot \ln E), \ln C \cdot A))$		142	.841

Regressions with 142 observations delete those with no children to permit logs.

having an average of zero children. (The linear form was rerun on the 142 observations for comparison.) In all the various forms, the income elasticity was less than unity—ranging from 0.340 to 0.499 (or higher when the education dummies were used). The education effect was negative, as expected, in all cases,[16] and the implied elasticity of consumption income, ϵ_{Y_cE}, considerably higher here than the average estimate from either Chapter 4 or 5. The education effect is stronger at lower levels of education, as seen from the three dummies that reflect the marginal effect of high school, college, and postgraduate schooling, respectively. The age effect is consistently negative, while nonwhites and Southerners have more children, ceteris paribus.

Considerable caution should be exercised in interpreting these results for children. First, the dependent variable is not the number of children ever born or raised by the household, but, rather, the number of children under eighteen. This explains the observed effect of age, since, obviously, older households have fewer young children. Second, the direction of causation between the dependent variable and the total consumption expenditure is not clear. While the number of children desired or demanded may rise with permanent income, total consumption expenditures probably rise as a result of increases in family size. This helps explain why the observed income elasticity from these regressions is higher than that ordinarily found for children. Clearly, much more work is required on this topic, and the results shown in this section are only suggestive.

---

[16] A possible alternative interpretation of the education coefficient could be that E is acting as a proxy for the opportunity cost of the wife's time and is therefore positively correlated with the price of children. This interpretation could also be made for the general consumption categories discussed previously, but relative "foregone earnings intensities" and relative substitution elasticities in production would determine relative price effects, and in the absence of some information on their magnitudes, such a model has no predictive ability. As additional knowledge is acquired about nonmarket production this analysis may be modified. As a first step our model appears capable of interpreting—and predicting—much of the observed behavior. (A difficulty which arises with this opportunity cost approach regarding the interpretation of the C variable was mentioned in Chapter 4, footnote 15.)

7

Summary

THIS STUDY IS related to the general topic of "returns" on an investment in human capital. Human capital is typically viewed as an asset which is acquired by an individual in the form of investment in training, health, information about markets, et cetera. The asset is embedded in the individual and yields a flow of productive services jointly with the use of his available time. Considerable evidence suggests a positive relationship between the level of one's stock of human capital—measured, say, by years of schooling—and one's level of earnings. From this relationship the monetary returns through the labor market are estimated.

If human capital yields a flow of productive services with manhours in the labor market, it may also yield a flow of services jointly with the time spent in other activities. Certain examples seem obvious: Some education yields productive services jointly with time spent reading books or balancing a checkbook; some improvements in health yield productive services jointly with time spent participating in sports; some investment in information about local markets yields productive services jointly with time spent shopping, and so forth. If general forms of human capital yield such services jointly with time spent outside the labor market (in the "nonmarket" sector), these services should also be considered as a "return" on the investment in human capital. These are the returns on which this study focuses.

The theory employs the concept of household production functions. The household is viewed as a small multiproduct firm in which its members' nonmarket time is combined with purchased market goods and services to produce commodities. The household consumes all of its own production of these commodities and thereby derives its utility. This production of commodities in the nonmarket sector responds to changes in the household's income and relative prices in the same manner as production of goods in the market sector responds to changes in income and relative prices.

In this context, the effects of changes in human capital operate through the nonmarket production functions, altering the parameters of the functions or the effective level of direct inputs, and thereby affecting the efficiency with which nonmarket production takes place. If the change enhances productivity in the nonmarket sector, the consumption "return" on the human capital is said to be positive. The model explores in some detail the changes in relative prices of different commodities resulting from unequal (or nonneutral) effects of human capital on the productivity of nonmarket production functions. It also analyzes the effects on real full income of shifts in overall production efficiency.

Chapter 2 analyzes one form of human capital, education. It shows that if education has an equiproportionate (or technologically "neutral") effect on all the nonmarket production functions, relative prices of commodities will be unaffected, while the household's income in real terms will change proportionately. In order to implement the model empirically with available data, the assumption is made that education has such a neutral effect across all production functions in the nonmarket sector. With this assumption the direction and magnitude of the effect can be inferred from observed shifts in the derived demand for factors of production—such as market goods and services—without directly observing the commodities produced.

The primary empirical work involves estimating cross-sectional income-expenditure curves for various categories of total consumption. The explanatory variables are the household's total consumption expenditure (used as a measure of its permanent money income), the education of the head of the household, the age of the head, the family's size, and its geographical region (South–non-South). From these modified Engel curves the household's responses to changes in money income and to changes in education level are estimated for each of the consumption items studied. From these observed income and education elasticities, an estimate of the magnitude and direction of the effect of education on nonmarket productivity can be computed; that is, knowing the magnitude of the household's response to changes in its money income and the magnitude of the response to changes in its educational level, one can infer the corresponding change in income that would induce the observed response resulting from the education change. The household is then said to behave as if its real income had changed by that corresponding amount, which is, in turn, attributed to education as its nonmarket productivity effect.

The principal data source was the Bureau of Labor Statistics' 1960–61 consumer expenditures survey. Chapter 4 used these data at a fairly broad level of aggregation to study the shifts in expenditure patterns over slightly more than a dozen consumption categories, as well as the shifts between the two broad categories of goods and services. For the goods-services dichotomy the evidence, interpreted by the model developed here, suggests that the effect of education on nonmarket productivity is a positive one. That is, the income elasticities indicate that, other things held constant including education, households with higher levels of income spend proportionately more of their total expenditure on services and that, other things held constant including money income, households with higher levels of education also spend proportionately more of their fixed total expenditure on services. Thus, those with more education behave as if they had more real income, despite the fact that their permanent money income is held constant. This is interpreted as evidence that the higher level of education enhances their capacity to produce useful commodities from a given level of factor inputs in the nonmarket sector.

The statistical analysis of the smaller categories of consumption—food at home, housefurnishings, clothing, and so forth—indicates that for ten of the fifteen items, the expenditures shift in the same manner with education as with money income. For the remaining items, or about 40 per cent of the total expenditure, the shifts are in opposite directions. Over the whole set of fifteen items, the average effect is a positive one regardless of how the effect is calculated, but the magnitude of the effect is small. By one measure (obtained from a weighted regression across items) the overall effect is +0.08 in elasticity terms, which implies that for a family whose head of the household has ten years of schooling and whose total family income is $10,000 per year, an additional year of schooling would contribute the equivalent of $80.00 through improved nonmarket efficiency. However, from another measure (obtained by imposing the neutrality constraint on the system of equations) the overall effect is about +0.70, which implies a consumption income effect that is considerably larger. By comparison, the effect of education on the total expenditure or money income was estimated to be about +0.80 in elasticity terms.

These estimates are crude, of course, and the results should not be taken as more than "ball park" point estimates of the effect of education on income through the nonmarket sector. Using the level of schooling of the household's head as the explanatory variable is itself only an approximation of the family members' amount of education. Likewise, separate analyses within specific age intervals could more adequately identify the important interaction effects that may exist. An additional problem is suggested in Appendix B, which shows that certain measurement errors may impose a negative correlation on the income and education elasticities, biasing the implied productivity effect downward. Finally, the simplifying assumption of technological neutrality is imposed at some cost on a system which clearly reflects some nonneutrality. Despite this, the model appears relatively effective for predicting the observed effects of education on expenditure patterns. It offers an internally consistent interpretation of these effects, and the order of magnitude of the implied elasticity of consumption income seems intuitively plausible. Furthermore, additional estimates of this elasticity discussed in the text and appendices are corroborative.

Chapter 5 disaggregates the 1960 expenditure data into much finer detail and analyzes the expenditure patterns across forty-five consumption items. Here, too, the estimates of education's effect on real full income through nonmarket productivity are positive, and when estimated by weighted regression across items, the elasticity estimate is again around $+ 0.10$. When the elasticity was estimated by iteration with the neutrality constraint imposed, the estimate was again around $+ 0.7$. The consistency of these estimates from the 1960 survey— whether based on fifteen or forty-five expenditure categories—is reassuring, since the permutations of functional forms, definitions of expenditure items, handling of zero expenditures, and so forth make it difficult to specify which estimate might be the most appropriate one.

Because of the difficulty in dealing with current expenditures on durable goods, the implied effect of education on real income was also estimated from a subset of thirty-five nondurable items taken from the forty-five just discussed. It was shown that biases related to durable goods expenditures could lower the estimate of education's nonmarket productivity effect. The regression estimate obtained from the nondurables alone was, indeed, higher, at approximately $+ 0.35$. When the neutrality constraint was imposed, the iterative procedure implied an elasticity in the vicinity of $+ 0.50$.

Chapter 6 discusses three different pieces of evidence related to the model. The first is an analysis of expenditure patterns from the 1950

Bureau of Labor Statistics survey similar to the 1960 data. For this body of data fifteen expenditure categories were used, and the point estimate of the education effect on real income was $+ 0.05$, expressed as an elasticity. The second section of Chapter 6 offers the model's explanation for previously observed differences in consumption patterns among immigrants in Israel from two studies of Israeli family expenditure patterns. The third briefly looks at some evidence relating to the demand for children in the context of the model. In addition, Appendices C and D present further evidence from the 1960 and 1950 Bureau of Labor Statistics surveys on expenditure patterns, indicating the extent to which the overall results discussed in Chapters 4, 5, and 6 are influenced by (or insensitive to) some aspects of the empirical procedures followed. For example, the zero expenditures are deleted, the education variable is replaced by three education dummy variables, the current total consumption expenditure variable is redefined, and so forth, and various estimates are presented with these changes. The force of this additional evidence supports the estimate of a small positive effect of education on real income through the nonmarket sector, as discussed in Chapter 4 and Chapter 5.

It should be stressed that this paper offers just one explanation for the empirical observation that education has an influence on consumer behavior aside from its role in market earnings and that this influence is essentially a systematic one. The explanation (presented in the theoretical chapters) around which the empirical results are centered rests on the effect of education on the productivity of household production functions. Other interpretations of the observed shifts in expenditure patterns can, of course, be suggested and several are discussed throughout the study. One of these, for example, suggests that education shifts preferences in a specified manner, while another discusses the results in the context of the effects of changes in the price of time. Distinguishing empirically among these and other alternative models will be facilitated by additional evidence. The model developed here is limited by the data to implications obtained from a relatively simple analysis under conditions of technological neutrality. But by its nature the model emphasizes the importance of substitution effects that would result from any nonneutrality in nonmarket production; it may ultimately be in interpreting these effects that its relative advantage lies.

For the present, the model appears reasonably capable of predicting the observed effects of education on expenditure patterns without any ad hoc assumptions. (Indeed, an effort is made in the text to avoid

the temptation of explaining the nonneutral cases on an ad hoc basis.)
More generally, the implications of the model in Chapter 1 are not
limited to effects of education, or human capital, on consumption expenditure patterns. Not only are there analogous implications for time
expenditures, for example, but the approach would also seem to be
applicable to the study of any other variables that affect the environ-
ment in which nonmarket production takes place.

Appendix A

1. MAXIMIZING THE HOUSEHOLD'S UTILITY

Given the utility function (1.1) and the production function (1.2), we may write

$$U = u[f_1(x_1, t_1; H), \ldots, f_n(x_n, t_n; H)], \tag{A.1}$$

and the time and money income constraints (1.3) and (1.4) can be combined as

$$Y_m = w(t - \sum_i t_i) + v = \sum x_i p_{x_i}$$

$$= wt + v - w\sum_i t_i,$$

with

$$Y_c = w\sum_i t_i = \sum_i t_i p_{t_i}$$

$$Y = Y_m + Y_c = wt + v = \sum_i (x_i p_{x_i} + t_i p_{t_i}). \tag{A.2}$$

To maximize (A.1) subject to (A.2), the Lagrangian

$$L = u[f_1(x_1, t_1; H), \ldots, f_n(x_n, t_n; H)] - \lambda[\sum_i (x_i p_{x_i} - t_i p_{t_i}) - Y] \tag{A.3}$$

is differentiated with respect to each factor x_i and t_i:

$$\frac{\partial L}{\partial x_i} = \frac{\partial u}{\partial f_i}\frac{\partial f_i}{\partial x_i} - \lambda p_{x_i} = 0,$$

which may be written as

$$MU_{z_i} \cdot MP_{x_i} - \lambda p_{x_i} = 0,$$

or the marginal utility of income, λ, is

$$\lambda = \frac{MU_{z_i} MP_{x_i}}{p_{x_i}}. \tag{A.4}$$

Since (A.4) holds for all factors, the usual equilibrium condition emerges:

$$\frac{MP_{x_i}}{p_{x_i}} = \frac{MP_{t_i}}{p_{t_i}} = \frac{\lambda}{MU_{Z_i}} = \frac{1}{MC_{Z_i}}. \tag{A.5}$$

2. THE COMMODITY PRICE

Defining the average price of a specific commodity Z as $\Pi = (p_x x + p_t t)/Z$ and substituting from (A.4) for p_x and p_t,

$$\Pi = \left[\left(\frac{MU_Z MP_x}{\lambda}\right)x + \left(\frac{MU_Z MP_t}{\lambda}\right)t\right]\bigg/Z$$

$$= \left(\frac{MU_Z}{\lambda}\right)\left(\frac{MP_x x + MP_t t}{Z}\right).$$

If the production functions are homogeneous of degree n, from Euler's theorem and (A.5)

$$\Pi = MC\left(\frac{nZ}{Z}\right),$$

so in equilibrium for commodity Z_i

$$\Pi_i = MC_i n. \tag{A.6}$$

This development of (A.6) also implies

$$\lambda = \frac{MU_Z n}{\Pi}, \tag{A.7}$$

and combining (A.4) with (A.7),

$$\frac{\lambda}{MU_Z} = \frac{MP_x}{p_x} = \frac{n}{\Pi}$$

or

$$p_x = \frac{MP_x \Pi}{n}. \tag{A.8}$$

From (A.8) it is clear that production shares, $w_x = (MP_x x/nZ)$, and expenditure shares, $s_x = (p_x x/\Pi Z)$, are equivalent:

$$\frac{p_x x}{\Pi Z} = \frac{(MP_x \Pi / n) x}{\Pi Z} = \frac{MP_x x}{nZ}. \tag{A.9}$$

3. THE EFFECT OF H ON PRODUCTIVITY AND THE COMMODITY PRICE

The effect of H on the output of Z_i, with the level of the inputs held fixed, would be some average of its effect on the productivity of the factors. For a homogeneous production function:

$$Z = (xMP_x + tMP_t)/n$$

$$\frac{dZ}{dH}\Big|_{x,\,t} = MP_{z^H} = \left(x \frac{\partial MP_x}{\partial H} + t \frac{\partial MP_t}{\partial H} \right) \Big/ n$$

$$\widetilde{MP}_i = \frac{MP_{z^H}}{Z} = \left(\frac{xMP_x}{nZ} \right) \widetilde{MP}_x + \left(\frac{tMP_t}{nZ} \right) \widetilde{MP}_t$$

for commodity Z_i, hence

$$\widetilde{MP}_i = \sum_f w_f \widetilde{MP}_f, \tag{A.10}$$

where f is an index over the factors of production. If, instead, we allow the quantities of the inputs to change, from (1.2),

$$dZ = MP_x dx + MP_t dt,$$

and dividing by dH and Z

$$\widetilde{Z} = \left(\frac{MP_x x}{Z} \right) \widetilde{x} + \left(\frac{MP_t t}{Z} \right) \widetilde{t}$$

$$\widetilde{Z} = (w_x \widetilde{x} + w_t \widetilde{t}) \, n, \tag{A.11}$$

i.e., a one per cent increase in x and t leads to an n per cent increase in Z. Equation (A.10) shows the direct effect of H on Z through its effect on the marginal products; equation (A.11) shows the indirect effect of H on Z through the induced changes in the quantities of the inputs.

The effect of H on the price of the commodity, Π, may be evaluated as follows. With the factor prices and the level of output held fixed, the differential is

$$d\Pi\Big|_{p_x,\ p_t,\ Z} = \left(\frac{p_x}{Z}\right) dx + \left(\frac{p_t}{Z}\right) dt,$$

so

$$\frac{d\Pi}{dH}\Big|_{p_x,\ p_t,\ Z} = \frac{p_x}{Z}\frac{dx}{dH} + \frac{p_t}{Z}\frac{dt}{dH}.$$

To evaluate dx/dH, sum (A.10) and (A.11) and set the sum equal to zero, which then holds the level of output constant, and solve for $\tilde{x}$:

$$\widetilde{MP}_i + (w_x\tilde{x} + w_t\tilde{t})n = 0$$

$$\tilde{x} = \frac{-\widetilde{MP}_i}{nw_x} - \frac{w_t}{w_x}\tilde{t}$$

or

$$\frac{dx}{dH} = -\frac{\widetilde{MP}_ix}{nw_x} - \frac{w_tx}{w_xt}\frac{dt}{dH}.$$

Substituting for dx/dH in $(d\Pi/dH)|p_x,\ p_t,\ Z$ for commodity i,

$$\frac{d\Pi_i}{dH} = \frac{p_x}{Z_i}\left(-\frac{\widetilde{MP}_ix}{w_xn} - \frac{w_tx}{w_xt}\frac{dt}{dH}\right) + \frac{p_t}{Z_i}\frac{dt}{dH}$$

and from (A.9)[1]

$$\tilde{\Pi}_i = \frac{-\widetilde{MP}_i}{n}. \tag{A.12}$$

From (A.6)

$$d\Pi_i = (dMC_i)\,n$$

$$\frac{d\Pi_i}{\Pi_i} = \frac{dMC_i}{\Pi_i}\,n = \frac{dMC_i}{MC_i},$$

so

[1] If $\tilde{\Pi}$ is, instead, evaluated holding the level of the inputs and the factor prices and the degree of homogeneity fixed, n drops out of the expression:

$$\widetilde{\Pi}_i = \widetilde{M}C_i. \tag{A.13}$$

4. THE PRICE LEVEL

Define the price level Π as

$$\Pi = \Pi_1^{s_1} \Pi_2^{s_2} \Pi_3^{s_3} \ldots \Pi_n^{s_n}$$

where the weights are the expenditure shares, then

$$\ln \Pi = \sum s_i \ln \Pi_i$$

or[2]

$$\widetilde{\Pi} = \frac{d \ln \Pi}{dH} = \sum_i s_i \widetilde{\Pi}_i. \tag{A.14}$$

5. THE DEMAND FOR THE COMMODITY AND THE INPUTS

If the demand for the commodity Z_i is written

$$Z_i^d = d_i \left(\frac{Y}{\Pi}, \frac{\Pi_i}{\Pi} \right) \tag{A.15}$$

$$\Pi = (p_x x + p_t t) / Z$$

$$\frac{d\Pi}{dH}\bigg|_{p_x, p_t, x, t} = - \left(\frac{\Pi Z}{Z^2} \right) \frac{dZ}{dH}\bigg|_{x, t},$$

$$\widetilde{\Pi} = - \widetilde{M} P_i \, .$$

[2] An alternative derivation of (A.14) uses an arithmetic price index. Let 0 represent a base level of H and 1 a unit increase in H. Defining each price relative to its base price and using base expenditure weights, the price index is

$$\pi^* = \sum_i s_i \frac{\pi_i^1}{\pi_i^0}; \, s_i = \frac{\pi_i^0 Z_i^0}{Y^0}; \sum_i s_i = 1.$$

Then the price index for the base level is unity

$$1 = \pi_0^* = \sum_i s_i \frac{\pi_i^0}{\pi_i^0}$$

$$d\pi^* = \pi_1^* - \pi_0^* = \sum_i s_i \frac{\pi_i^1 - \pi_i^0}{\pi_i^0} = \sum_1 s_i \frac{d\pi_i}{\pi_i^0}$$

so

$$\frac{d\pi^*}{dH} = \sum_i s_i \frac{d\pi_i}{dH}\bigg|_{\pi_i^0} = \sum_i s_i \widetilde{\pi}_i$$

then the effect of an increase in H on $Z_i{}^d$ can be derived from the total differential[3]

$$dZ_i{}^d = \frac{\partial Z}{(\partial Y/\Pi)} d(Y/\Pi) + \frac{\partial Z}{\partial(\Pi_i/\Pi)} d(\Pi_i/\Pi)$$

$$\widetilde{Z}_i{}^d = \frac{dZ_i{}^d}{dH}\bigg|_{} Z_i{}^d = \left(\frac{\partial Z_i}{\partial(Y/\Pi)} \frac{(Y/\Pi)}{Z}\right)\left(\frac{d(Y/\Pi)}{dH} \frac{1}{(Y/\Pi)}\right)$$

$$+ \left(\frac{\partial Z}{\partial(\Pi_i/\Pi)} \frac{d(\Pi_i/\Pi)}{dH} \frac{1}{(\Pi_i/\Pi)}\right)$$

$$\widetilde{Z}_i{}^d = \eta_i\left(\frac{\widetilde{Y}}{\Pi}\right) + \epsilon_i\left(\frac{\widetilde{\Pi}_i}{\Pi}\right), \tag{A.16}$$

where η_i and ϵ_i are the commodity's income and own-price elasticity and

$$(Y\widetilde{/}\Pi) = \widetilde{Y} - \widetilde{\Pi}; \; (\Pi_i\widetilde{/}\Pi) = \widetilde{\Pi}_i - \widetilde{\Pi}.[4]$$

Substituting from (1.13), the equation (A.16) can be written as

$$\widetilde{Z}_i{}^d = \eta_i(\widetilde{Y} + \widetilde{Y}_c) + \epsilon_i(\widetilde{\Pi}_i - \widetilde{\Pi}). \tag{A.17}$$

For the factor x, used in the production of a commodity,

$$Z_i = f_i(x_i, t_i; H),$$

so

$$\frac{dZ}{dH} = \frac{\partial Z}{\partial x} \frac{dx}{dH} + \frac{\partial Z}{\partial t} \frac{dt}{dH} + \frac{dZ}{dH}\bigg|_{x, t,}$$

where the left-hand term is the gross or total effect of H on Z de-

---

or

$$\widetilde{\pi}^* = \sum_i s_i \widetilde{\pi}_i.$$

[3] More generally, if $Z_i{}^d = d_i(Y/\Pi, \Pi_j/\Pi)$ for j from 1 to n,

$$\widetilde{Z}_i{}^d = \eta_i\left(\frac{\widetilde{Y}}{\Pi}\right) + \sum_j \epsilon_{ij}\left(\frac{\widetilde{\Pi}_j}{\Pi}\right)$$

where ϵ_{ij} represents own- and cross-price elasticities.

[4] Since $\widetilde{\Pi}$ is defined holding p_i fixed (see the development of (A.12)), to be consistent:

manded and the final term is the change in the Z produced, with the factors held constant. Dividing by Z and letting $n = 1$,

$$\widetilde{Z}^d = \left(\frac{MP_x x}{Z}\right)\widetilde{x} + w_t\widetilde{t} + \widetilde{MP}_i,$$

since $\partial Z/\partial x = MP_x$, and where $\widetilde{MP}_i$ is defined in (A.10). Since $w_x = (1 - w_t)$,

$$\widetilde{Z}^d = \widetilde{x} - w_t(\widetilde{x} - \widetilde{t}) + \widetilde{MP}_i,$$

so

$$\widetilde{x} = \widetilde{Z}^d - \widetilde{MP}_i + w_t(\widetilde{x} - \widetilde{t}). \tag{A.18}$$

Now, making use of the assumption of linear homogeneity of the production function and permitting factor nonneutrality,

$$MP_r = \phi(f_r, H),$$

where MP_r is the ratio of marginal products (MP_x/MP_t) and f_r is the ratio of factors of production (x/t). Then

$$\frac{dMP_r}{dH} = \frac{\partial MP_r}{\partial f_r}\frac{df_r}{dH} + \frac{\partial MP_r}{\partial H}$$

or

$$\widetilde{Y} = \frac{d(wt_m + V)}{dH}\bigg/Y = \frac{t_m w}{Y}\widetilde{w} + \frac{V}{Y}\widetilde{V},$$

i.e., Y is the effect of H on real full income through market earnings and property income. If, instead, $\widetilde{\Pi}^*$ allowed p_i to vary,

$$\widetilde{\Pi}^* = \widetilde{\Pi} + \sum_i \left(\frac{t_i p_{t_i}}{Y}\right)\widetilde{p}_{t_i},$$

and since $p_{t_i} = w$,

$$\widetilde{\Pi}^* = \widetilde{\Pi} + \frac{(\Sigma t_i)w}{Y}\widetilde{w} = \widetilde{\Pi} + \frac{t_c w}{Y}\widetilde{w}.$$

In this case $\widetilde{Y}^* = (tw/Y)\widetilde{w} + (V/Y)\widetilde{V}$ and the term $(t_c w/Y)\widetilde{w}$ will net itself out of $(\widetilde{Y}^* - \widetilde{\Pi}^*)$.

Notice, too, that if Y were to include a term $(wt_w/Y)\widetilde{t}_m$ (i.e., a shift of hours into or from the market), the consumption income term would also include a term $(wt_c/Y)\widetilde{t}_c$, and since $(dt_c/dH) = -dt_m/dH)$, these two terms will also net themselves out.

$$\frac{dMP_r}{dH} \frac{1}{MP_r} = \frac{-1}{\sigma} (\tilde{x} - \tilde{\imath}) + (\tilde{M}P_x - \tilde{M}P_\iota),$$

where the left-hand side shows the gross or total effect of H on the ratio of marginal products after the factor substitution, and σ is the elasticity of substitution in production, defined to be positive. Since in equilibrium $MP_r = p_x/p_t$,

$$dMP_r/MP_r = d(p_x/p_\iota)/(p_x/p_\iota).$$

So

$$\tilde{p}_x - \tilde{p}_\iota = \frac{-1}{\sigma} (\tilde{x} - \tilde{\imath}) + (\tilde{M}P_x - \tilde{M}P_\iota). \tag{A.19}$$

Substituting $(\tilde{x} - \tilde{\imath})$ from (A.19) and substituting for $\tilde{Z}_i{}^d$ from (A.17) into (A.18) and rearranging,

$$\tilde{x} = \eta_i(\tilde{Y} + \tilde{Y}_c) - \tilde{M}P_i + \epsilon_i(\tilde{\Pi}_i - \tilde{\Pi}) \\ + w_\iota \sigma(\tilde{M}P_x - \tilde{M}P_\iota) - w_\iota \sigma(\tilde{p}_x - \tilde{p}_\iota). \tag{A.20}$$

These terms represent, respectively, the gross income effect, the direct productivity effect, the substitution in consumption effect, and the substitution in production effect (through H's effect on relative marginal products and relative factor prices). If x is evaluated holding money income and factor prices fixed, equation (A.20) reduces to

$$\tilde{x} = \eta_i\tilde{Y}_c - \tilde{M}P_i + \epsilon_i(\tilde{\Pi}_i - \tilde{\Pi}) + w_\iota\sigma(\tilde{M}P_x - \tilde{M}P_\iota). \tag{A.21}$$

6. THE PRODUCTIVITY MODEL AND UTILITY

In this section the productivity model is couched in terms of utility, and it is shown that the relative increase in the demand for a commodity is greater the larger its relative utility elasticity. From the utility function (A.1), the marginal utility of the environmental variable H is simply:

$$\frac{\partial U}{\partial H} = \frac{\partial U}{\partial f_1}\frac{\partial f_1}{\partial H} + \frac{\partial U}{\partial f_2}\frac{\partial f_2}{\partial H} + \ldots + \frac{\partial U}{\partial f_n}\frac{\partial f_n}{\partial H} = \sum_i \frac{\partial U}{\partial f_i}\frac{\partial f_i}{\partial H} = \sum_i \frac{\tilde{Z}}{\mu_i} U,$$

where $\mu_i = (\partial Z_i/\partial U)U/Z_i$ is a utility elasticity of commodity Z_i.[5] Expressed in percentage terms per unit change in H,

$$\tilde{U} = \frac{\partial U}{\partial H}\frac{1}{U} = \sum \frac{\tilde{Z_i}}{\mu_i}. \tag{A.22}$$

Equation (A.22) will be positive if the environmental variable increases the output of all Z's (holding the direct inputs, x and t, constant) and if the commodities are "normal goods." H's effect on total utility is simply the sum of its indirect effect on utility through each commodity, measured in comparable units.

To determine how this might affect the quantities demanded of the Z's, rewrite (A.15) as a function of total utility (an alternative measure of the opportunity constraint) and relative prices,

$$Z_i^d = d_i\left(U, \frac{\Pi_i}{\Pi}\right), \tag{A.23}$$

or relative to some other commodity Z_j,

$$\left(\frac{Z_i}{Z_j}\right)^d = h\left(U, \frac{\Pi_i}{\Pi_j}\right). \tag{A.24}$$

From (A.24) the effect of H on the relative demand for the commodities is

$$\left(\frac{\tilde{Z_i}}{Z_j}\right)^d = (\mu_i - \mu_j)\tilde{U} - \sigma\left(\frac{\tilde{\Pi_i}}{\Pi_j}\right), \tag{A.25}$$

where σ is the elasticity of substitution in consumption

$$\sigma = \frac{-\partial Z_i/Z_j}{\partial \Pi_i/\Pi_j}\frac{\Pi_i Z_j}{\Pi_j Z_i}.$$

If H's productivity effect is biased toward Z_i relative to Z_j,

$$(\widetilde{\Pi_i/\Pi_j}) = \tilde{\Pi}_i - \tilde{\Pi}_j < 0,$$

[5] The utility elasticity of a commodity is identically equal to the ratio of its income elasticity to the elasticity of total utility with respect to income:

$$\mu_i = \frac{\partial Z_i}{\partial U}\frac{U}{Z_i} = \frac{\partial Z_i}{\partial U}\frac{U}{Z_i}\frac{\partial Y}{\partial Y}\frac{Y}{Y} = \left(\frac{\partial Z_i}{\partial Y}\frac{Y}{Z_i}\right)\bigg/\left(\frac{\partial U}{\partial Y}\frac{Y}{U}\right) = \frac{\eta_i}{\epsilon_{UY}}$$

where ϵ_{UY} is presumably positive. The ratio of utility elasticities of two items is then equal to the ratio of their income elasticities, and the absolute difference is:

$$(\mu_i - \mu_j) = (\eta_i - \eta_j)\frac{1}{\epsilon_{UY}}.$$

provided H reduces the prices of the commodities. Then the second term in (A.25) is positive $(-\sigma(\widetilde{\Pi_i/\Pi_i}) > 0)$ and tends to make $\widetilde{Z}_i{}^d > \widetilde{Z}_j{}^d$ (which is the usual case for a decline in the relative price of Z_i). If H is presumed to be commodity neutral, (A.25) reduces to:

$$(Z_i\widetilde{/Z_j})^d = (\mu_i - \mu_j)\widetilde{U}. \tag{A.26}$$

Equation (A.26) suggests the effect on the relative demand for Z_i of the expansion in opportunities (or utility). If $\widetilde{U}$ is positive, then

$$\widetilde{Z}_i{}^d \gtreqless \widetilde{Z}_j{}^d \quad \text{when} \quad \mu_i \gtreqless \mu_j.$$

That is, the change in the demand for Z_i is relatively great when Z_i's elasticity is relatively large. From footnote 5 above, (A.26) can also be expressed as

$$(Z_i\widetilde{/Z_j})^d = \widetilde{Z}_i{}^d - \widetilde{Z}_j{}^d = (\eta_i - \eta_j)\frac{\widetilde{U}}{\epsilon_{UY}} \tag{A.27}$$

and since $(\widetilde{U}/\epsilon_{UY}) > 0$, the relative demand for Z_i is greater the larger its (relative) income elasticity. Equation (A.27) again emphasizes the fact that, were the utility function homogeneous (i.e., were all income elasticities unity), there would be no effect on the relative demand for commodities resulting from a neutral productivity shift.

Equation (A.27) must imply the same relationship as was discussed previously, since, after all, it is simply a translation of that discussion. For example, if we write (A.16) for two commodities and consider their difference,

$$(\widetilde{Z}_i{}^d - \widetilde{Z}_j{}^d) = (\eta_i - \eta_j)\left(\frac{\widetilde{Y}}{\Pi}\right) + (\epsilon_i\widetilde{\Pi}_i - \epsilon_j\widetilde{\Pi}_j) - \widetilde{\Pi}(\epsilon_i - \epsilon_j), \tag{A.28}$$

and if $\widetilde{\Pi}_i = \widetilde{\Pi}_j = \widetilde{\Pi}$,

$$(\widetilde{Z}_i{}^d - \widetilde{Z}_j{}^d) = (\eta_i - \eta_j)(\widetilde{Y}/\Pi), \tag{A.29}$$

which equated to (A.27) implies:

$$(\widetilde{Y}/\Pi) = (\widetilde{U}/\epsilon_{UY}), \tag{A.30}$$

where the income term in ϵ_{UY} is understood to be in real terms.

7. A "CHANGE IN TASTES" INTERPRETATION

The previous section expressed the productivity model in terms of an effect on behavior through a change in the level of utility. But since the utility level was presumed to be affected by the increased non-market productivity, that section did not really offer an alternative way of viewing the effect of H on behavior. This section does so by suggesting that H affects the utility level directly, not through productivity but simply by changing the indifference map; that is, by changing tastes.

Specifically, consider the case of two commodities, Z_L, a luxury, and Z_N, a necessity, and suppose

$$MU_L/MU_N = g(Z_L/Z_N, U), \tag{A.31}$$

i.e., where the ratio of marginal utilities depends upon the level of total utility as well as upon the ratio of the commodities (or, the utility function is not homogeneous). Now, if H affects the total level of utility directly, then it indirectly affects (MU_L/MU_N) both through U and the induced change in (Z_L/Z_N). Letting A represent (MU_L/MU_N) and B represent (Z_L/Z_N):

$$\frac{dA}{dH} = \frac{\partial A}{\partial B}\frac{dB}{dH} + \frac{\partial A}{\partial U}\frac{dU}{dH}\bigg|_{x,\,t} \tag{A.32}$$

or

$$\widetilde{A} = \frac{-1}{\sigma}(\widetilde{B}) + \epsilon_{AU}\widetilde{U}, \tag{A.33}$$

where σ is the elasticity of substitution in consumption ($\sigma > 0$) and ϵ_{AU} is the elasticity of (MU_L/MU_N) with respect to U.

The terms in (A.33) can be evaluated as follows. The effect on the ratio of the marginal utilities of an increase in (Z_L/Z_N), holding U constant, is:

$$\frac{\partial A}{\partial B} = \left(\frac{\partial MU_L}{\partial B}\frac{1}{MU_L} - \frac{\partial MU_N}{\partial B}\frac{1}{MU_N}\right)A$$

or

$$\frac{-1}{\sigma} = (\epsilon_{MU_LB} - \epsilon_{MU_NB}) < 0, \tag{A.34}$$

since the indifference curve is convex. Similarly, the effect on (MU_L/MU_N) of an increase in U, holding (Z_L/Z_N) fixed, would be:

$$\frac{\partial A}{\partial U} = \left(\frac{\partial MU_L}{\partial U}\frac{1}{MU_L} - \frac{\partial MU_N}{\partial U}\frac{1}{MU_N}\right) A > 0$$

or

$$\epsilon_{AU} = \frac{\partial A}{\partial U}\frac{U}{A} = (\epsilon_{MU_LU} - \epsilon_{MU_NU}) > 0. \tag{A.35}$$

Since Z_L is a luxury, along a ray the slope of the indifference curves (MU_L/MU_N) increases (the slope rises to the left and falls to the right of P, which is the locus of tangency points from a parallel shift in the budget constant in Figure A).

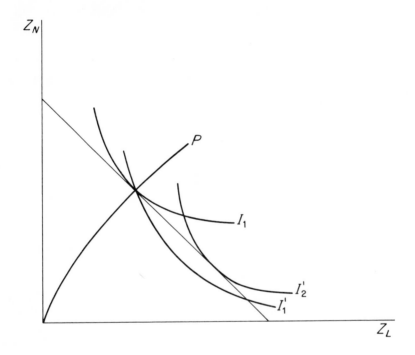

FIGURE A

Initially, as H rises and increases U (and before the induced change in (Z_L/Z_N) occurs), (MU_L/MU_N) rises, since $(\epsilon_{AU}\tilde{U})$ is positive. But since a change in H does not affect the price ratio (Π_L/Π_N), the equilibrium level of (MU_L/MU_N) must be unchanged. So, setting (A.33) to zero shows the induced effect on (Z_L/Z_N) of H's influence on U:

$$(\widetilde{Z_L/Z_N}) = \sigma\epsilon_{AU}\widetilde{U} > 0 \qquad (A.36)$$

and

$$\sigma\epsilon_{AU} = \frac{\partial B}{\partial U}\frac{U}{B} = (\mu_L - \mu_N) > 0, \qquad (A.37)$$

where μ_i is the utility elasticity defined in the previous section. Thus, we are left with

$$(\widetilde{Z_L/Z_N}) = (\mu_L - \mu_N)\widetilde{U} > 0,$$

as in the previous section. The interpretation here is that H raises the level of utility and in so doing raises the ratio (MU_L/MU_N), altering the indifference map from that represented by I_1 to that represented by I_1'. But since prices are unaffected, the initial combination of Z_L and Z_N is no longer an optimal one, and the new equilibrium contains relatively more of the luxury.

Appendix B

THE PURPOSE OF this appendix is to consider the biases that might exist in the estimated coefficients and to discuss the relationship of these biases to the model's prediction of a positive correlation between the estimated income and education elasticities.

1. THE STRUCTURE

Suppose a household's expenditure on a market good, X, is a function of its permanent money income, Y_p, and its nonmarket efficiency, E_f:[1]

$$X = \alpha + \beta_Y Y_p + \beta_{E_f} E_f + u, \qquad (B.1)$$

where u is an independent stochastic disturbance term. When fitted in the appropriate log form, β_Y is an estimate of the income elasticity of X and β_{E_f} is an estimate of the elasticity of expenditure on X with respect to nonmarket efficiency. We expect β_Y to be positive for most, if not all, of the market goods. The model developed here suggests that under certain specified assumptions, β_{E_f} will be positive, zero, or negative as β_Y is $\gtreqless$ unity.

Since neither Y_p nor E_f is directly observable, some proxy for each is used. We assume that total permanent consumption, C_p, is proportional to Y_p and that E_f is a function of the household's level of education, E, the age of its members, A, and a vector, V, of other factors including ability:

$$C_p = b_1 Y_p$$

or measured consumption, C, is

$$C = b_1 Y_p + C_t,$$

where C_t is transitory consumption, so

---

[1] The two other variables used in the empirical chapters, family size and region, add nothing of substance in the context of this appendix and will be ignored.

$$Y_p = (C - C_t)/b_1, \tag{B.2}$$

$$E_f = a_1 + a_2 E + a_3 A + a_4 V, \tag{B.3}$$

where b_1, a_2, and $a_4 > 0$ and the sign of a_3 is ambiguous. Substituting (B.2) and (B.3) into (B.1),

$$X = (\alpha + a_1\beta_{E_f}) + (\beta_Y/b_1)C + (\beta_{E_f}a_2)E + (\beta_{E_f}a_3)A$$
$$+ (u + \beta_{E_f}a_4 V - (\beta_Y/b_1)C_t)$$

or

$$X = \alpha^* + \beta_C^* C + \beta_E^* E + \beta_A^* A + w \tag{B.4}$$

where

$$w = u + \beta_{E_f}a_4 V - \beta_C^* C_t.$$

2. THE ESTIMATING EQUATION

If equation (B-4) is estimated empirically by ordinary least squares, the estimated equation would be

$$X = a + b_C C + b_E E + b_A A + \epsilon \tag{B.5}$$

for each consumption item. In matrix notation

$$X = Y\beta + w \tag{B.6}$$

where X is an n by 1 column vector of the n observations on the expenditure item, β is a 3 by 1 vector of the regression coefficients, w is an n by 1 vector of error terms, and

$$Y = \begin{pmatrix} C_1 \ E_1 \ A_1 \\ C_2 \ E_2 \ A_2 \\ \vdots \ \vdots \ \vdots \\ C_n \ E_n \ A_n \end{pmatrix}, \tag{B.7}$$

expressing the variables in deviation form. By the use of ordinary least squares

$$\hat{\beta} = (Y'Y)^{-1}(Y'X) \tag{B.8}$$

and the expected value of $\hat{\beta}$ can be expressed as

$$E(\hat{\beta}) = \beta + (Y'Y)^{-1}E(Y'w). \tag{B.9}$$

The variance-covariance matrix of $\hat{\beta}$ is

$$\text{var}(\hat{\beta}) = \sigma_w^2 (Y'Y)^{-1}, \tag{B.10}$$

and Haitovsky has shown that the elements in this matrix can be expressed in terms of the partial correlations between the independent variables:[2]

$$\text{cov} \ (\beta_i \beta_j) \ = \ - \ \rho_{ij.l} \, \sigma_{\beta_i} \sigma_{\beta_j}, \tag{B.11}$$

where l is an index over other independent variables, and $\rho_{ij.l}$ is the partial correlation coefficient of independent variables i and j. Thus the covariation between, say, the income elasticity and the education elasticity $(l \equiv A)$ is opposite in sign to the partial correlation of income and education. For $i = j$, (B.11) is an identity given the convention that the partial correlation coefficient of a variable with itself is minus one: $\rho_{ii.l} = -1$. So we may express the ijth element in $(Y'Y)^{-1}$ from (B.10) and (B.11) as

$$(Y'Y)_{ij}^{-1} \ = \ - \ \rho_{ij.l} k_{ij} \ \ \text{where} \ k_{ij} = \frac{\sigma_{\beta_i} \sigma_{\beta_j}}{\sigma_w^2} > 0; \text{ all } i, j. \tag{B.12}$$

That is, the sign of the ijth element in $(Y'Y)^{-1}$ is opposite the sign of $\rho_{ij.l}$.[3]

Writing out the three rows in (B.9) using (B.12):

$$\text{E}(b_C) = \beta_C^* + k_{CC}\text{E}(C'w) - \rho_{CE.A}k_{CE}\text{E}(E'w) - \rho_{CA.E}k_{CA}\text{E}(A'w)$$

$$\text{E}(b_E) = \beta_E^* - \rho_{EC.A}k_{EC}\text{E}(C'w) + k_{EE}\text{E}(E'w) - \rho_{EA.C}k_{EA}\text{E}(A'w)$$

$$\text{E}(b_A) = \beta_A^* - \rho_{AC.E}k_{AC}\text{E}(C'w) - \rho_{AE.C}k_{AE}\text{E}(E'w) + k_{AA}\text{E}(A'w). \tag{B.13}$$

To determine the direction of these effects we must know the partial correlation matrix and the sign of each of the expected value terms.

3. THE DIRECTION OF BIASES

We will assume that A is uncorrelated with u, C_t, and hence $\text{E}(A'w) = 0$ and the final term drops out of each line of (B.13). Writing out the remaining two terms,

[2] See Yoel Haitovsky, "On the Correlation Between Estimated Parameters in Linear Regressions," NBER, Mimeo., May 1969.

[3] From (B.10), var $(\hat{\beta})/\sigma_w^2 = (Y'Y)^{-1}$ and the ijth element would be

$$\frac{\text{cov} \ \beta_i \beta_j}{\sigma_w^2} \ = \ - \ \frac{\rho_{ij.l} \, \sigma_{\beta_i} \sigma_{\beta_j}}{\sigma_w^2} \ = \ - \ \rho_{ij.l} k_{ij}$$

If $i = j$, $k_{ij} = \sigma_{\beta_i}^2 / \sigma_w^2 > 0$ and since $\rho_{ij.l} = -1$, the term is necessarily positive. This must be the case, obviously, since it is a variance term on the principal diagonal.

$$E(C'w) = E[(C'u) + \beta_E \, a_4(C'V) - \beta_C^*(C'C_t)]$$

$$E(E'w) = E[(E'u) + \beta_{E_f}a_4(E'V) - \beta_C^*(E'C_t)]. \qquad (B.14)$$

It seems reasonable to suppose $(E'u) = (E'C_t) = 0$ and that $(E'V) > 0$, since education is positively correlated with ability. Hence with $a_4 > 0$ and β_{E_f} having the sign of $(\beta_C^* - 1)$:

$$E(E'w) = \beta_{E_f}a_4 E(E'V) \gtreqless 0 \quad \text{as } \beta_C^* \gtreqless 1. \qquad (B.15)$$

Next consider E $(C'w)$. Since $C = C_p + C_t$, $(C'C_t) = (C_p'C_t) + (C_t'C_t) = n\sigma_{C_t}^2$ by the usual assumption that C_t and C_p are uncorrelated. Likewise, $(C'V) = (C_p'V) + (C_t'V) = (C_p'V) > 0$, since the permanent component in income or consumption is presumably positively related to ability. Finally, since u is the transitory expenditure on the item in question and is therefore unrelated to C_p but is related to C_t by the definition $\sum_g u_{g_i} = C_{t_i}$ (where g is an index over consumption items for the ith observation), $(C'u) = (C_t'u) > 0$, unless the transitory expenditure on one item is offset by a negative transitory expenditure on another item in the consumption basket. In fact, it may be reasonable to suppose that $(C_t'u) = 0$ for most items except those on which expenditures tend to be lumpy, e.g., durable goods. Since an expenditure on a durable—an automobile, a major appliance, a home, et cetera—is probably not offset within the period, for these durables it seems very likely that $(C_t'u) > 0$. Summarizing these effects on $(C'w)$:

"durables" $E(C'u) > 0$ for durable items,

"ability" $\beta_{E_f}a_4 E(C'V) \gtreqless 0 \quad \text{as } \beta_C^* \gtreqless 1,$ $\left. \begin{array}{c} \\ \\ \\ \\ \end{array} \right\}$(B.16)

"measurement" $- \beta_C^* E(C'C_t) < 0$ for superior goods.

In order to determine the direction of the biases on the estimated coefficients, we must also know the partial correlations between the independent variables. These are given in the following table for the 1960 BLS data used in Chapters 4 and 5.[4]

---

[4] The matrix includes the two additional explanatory variables, family size and region, despite their being omitted from the discussion in this appendix.

Partial Correlation Matrix Weighted by $\sqrt{\text{Cell Size}}$

	ln E	A	F	R
ln C	.662	.299	.865	−.441
ln E		−.755	−.733	.102
A			−.591	−.002
F				.376

Equation (B.13) can now be rewritten, defining k^*_{ij} as $|\rho_{ij \cdot l}|k_{ij}$, which is always positive, and assigning the proper sign to each term from the partial correlation matrix:

$$\mathrm{E}(b_C) = \beta_C^* + k_{CC}\mathrm{E}(C'w) - k_{CE \cdot A}\mathrm{E}(E'w)$$

$$\mathrm{E}(b_E) = \beta_E^* - k^*_{EC \cdot A}\mathrm{E}(C'w) + k_{EE}\mathrm{E}(E'w) \qquad \text{(B.17)}$$

$$\mathrm{E}(b_A) = \beta_A^* - k^*_{AC \cdot E}\mathrm{E}(C'w) + k^*_{AE \cdot C}\mathrm{E}(E'w).$$

Several points can be made from equations (B.15)–(B.17). First, notice that the two "ability" biases work in opposite directions and may result in no net effect on the coefficients. The effect of $\mathrm{E}(C'V)$ on b_C is positive for a luxury, but the effect of $\mathrm{E}(E'V)$ for this case is negative;[5] similarly, the effects are opposite for necessities and for the education coefficient. Second, if we assume for the moment that $\mathrm{E}(C'V) = \mathrm{E}(E'V) = 0$ and focus on the measurement errors,

$$\mathrm{E}(C'w) = \mathrm{E}(C_t'u - \beta_C^* n \sigma_{C_t}^2),$$

so from (B.17)

$$\mathrm{E}(b_C) \gtrless \beta_C^* \quad \text{as} \quad \left(\frac{\mathrm{cov}(C_t u)}{\sigma_{C_t}^2}\right) \gtrless \beta_C^*, \qquad \text{(B.18)}$$

which is equivalent to the statement made by Liviatan,[6] and

$$\mathrm{E}(b_E) \lessgtr \beta_E^* \quad \text{as} \quad \left(\frac{\mathrm{cov}(C_t u)}{\sigma_{C_t}^2}\right) \gtrless \beta_C^*. \qquad \text{(B.19)}$$

---

[5] Isolating these "ability" biases on $\mathrm{E}(b_C)$, from (B.17):

$$\mathrm{E}(b_C) - \beta_C^* = (\beta_{Ef}a_4/\sigma_w^2)(\sigma_{\beta_C}^2\mathrm{E}(C'V) - |\rho_{CE \cdot l}| \sigma_{\beta_C}\sigma_{\beta_E}\mathrm{E}(E'V))$$

so the bias is positive, nonexistent, or negative as

$$(\sigma_{\beta_C}/\sigma_{\beta_E}|\rho_{CE \cdot l}|) \gtrless \mathrm{E}(E'V)/\mathrm{E}(C'V).$$

[6] Liviatan, "Errors in Variables," p. 338.

Since this covariance term is likely to be large for lumpy, durable expenditures, their income elasticities are likely to be biased upward, and their education elasticities biased downward.[7]

Notice here that the bias in one direction in the estimate of the income elasticity implies a bias in the opposite direction in the estimate of the education elasticity. And this is the case in general, given the positive partial correlation between income and education: an upward bias on the one coefficient is associated with a downward bias on the other coefficient.[8] Yet a positive relationship between these coefficients is implied by the theoretical model being tested here. If the income elasticities of durables, which tend to be luxuries according to estimates here and elsewhere, are biased upward and their education elasticities biased downward, these biases tend to impose a relationship on the coefficients opposite to that implied by the theory. Furthermore, since the weighted average of these elasticity estimates must be one and zero, respectively, if an upward bias exists in the luxuries, some other items, probably necessities, must be biased downward. Both of these, then, tend to impose a negative correlation on the elasticity estimates.[9]

Grouping the data, as was done for the empirical investigation in this study, should reduce these measurement error biases. The data were cross-classified by, among other things, measured income and education level, and group averages were used. This is the method suggested by Friedman for eliminating the transitory effects.[10] The

---

[7] From estimates of the relative biases on income coefficients, Liviatan states: "Upward biased elasticities are those of durables and clothing which are generally considered as 'unstable' or 'variable' items. On the other hand, rent, which can be considered as the most stable type of expenditure, exhibits the largest downward bias. These phenomena seem to be consistent with the analysis . . . which pointed out the relations between direction of bias and amount of random variability in a given expenditure item." Ibid., p. 343.

[8] This is related to Haitovsky's equation (see B.11), since, if $\rho_{CE.1} > 0$, the covariation between β_C and β_E is negative.

[9] If, instead, the income elasticities of luxuries were biased downward and those of necessities upward, then education elasticities of the former would be biased upward and those of the latter downward. In this case the biases alone would tend to produce empirical results that would "support" the model's prediction of a positive relationship between the elasticities across the items. It is fortuitous that the durables which are most likely to have income effects biased upward are also luxuries, for if the empirical results support the model it is in spite of, not as a result of, these measurement error biases.

[10] Friedman suggests, as a way of eliminating the influence of transitory factors affecting income, "to classify the families by measured income, to compute

same procedure was suggested by Liviatan. He shows that if measured income, Y, is highly correlated with permanent income and is not correlated with random elements in consumption, then grouping by measured income and using mean expenditures and mean total consumption eliminates the transitory bias. This is, in fact, the procedure used by Liviatan for much of his empirical work.[11]

Thus, the effect of the transitory components should be reduced by the grouping procedure used, although it need not be eliminated, especially in those cases in which the cell size is small.[12] There seems to be no reason to expect the grouping procedure to reduce also the influence of the two "ability" biases, but, as indicated above, these two work in opposite directions on all coefficients.[13]

4. THE TRADITIONAL ENGEL CURVE

Perhaps it should be stressed that some of the biases considered here result from our insistence on including as separate independent variables both the money income and the nonmarket efficiency of the household. Were we willing to combine these two into one variable

mean expenditures on an individual category of consumption and on all categories combined for each class. Under the relevant assumptions about correlations and mean transitory components of consumption, these means are estimates of the mean permanent components of the individual category and of total consumption. The relation between them is then an estimated relation between permanent components." Milton Friedman, *A Theory of the Consumption Function,* Princeton University Press for NBER, 1957, p. 207.

[11] See Nissan Liviatan, *Consumption Patterns in Israel,* Jerusalem, Falk Project for Economic Research in Israel, 1964, p. 78.

[12] Liviatan indicates that about fifty families per cell is "quite satisfactory" in this grouping method (ibid., p. 358). For my empirical work here, the 1960 data contained an average of nearly ninety households, although the 1950 data's average cell size was approximately fifty in Chapter 6 and is considerably smaller in Appendix D. Even for the 1960 data, since the cells were not of equal size, some had substantially fewer than fifty observations; hence the biases may not be fully eliminated.

[13] Notice that if V is uncorrelated with C_p but is correlated positively with education, then the resulting bias tends to support the model's prediction. But this particular circumstance might be considered legitimate supporting evidence in the sense that it indicates that ability or health or some other factor in V raises nonmarket efficiency ($a_4 > 0$). These effects should not, however, be attributed to formal schooling. But since these factors presumably also affect market efficiency, and hence C_p, the offsetting effects exist and the net effect may be negligible.

many of our problems would disappear. However, since the basic model suggests that human capital has an effect on consumption over and above its effect on money earnings or income, we wish to separate out these effects. If the model is accepted, it suggests that running Engel curves with only a money income variable, and omitting the productivity effect, creates a bias of another sort. This would be tantamount to fitting equation (B.1) while omitting the variable E_f. We know that the expected value of the coefficient from this simple regression $x = a + b_{Y_p}Y_p + e$, where $e = \beta_{E_f}E_f + u$, is

$$E(b_{Y_p}) = \beta_Y + \beta_{E_f}b_{E_f Y_p}, \tag{B.20}$$

where $b_{E_f Y_p}$ is the simple regression coefficient of E_f on Y_p, which is presumably positive in this case. Thus, our model suggests that this estimated coefficient b_{Y_p} is biased away from unity, since $\beta_Y \lessgtr 1$ implies $\beta_{E_f} \lessgtr 0$ from the model. That is, the income coefficient obtained in the traditional Engel curve includes both a money income effect and an efficiency effect, and so, for example, if human capital is correlated with E_f, but physical capital is not, then the estimated income coefficient would differ depending on which form of capital it resulted from. The income coefficient related to a return on financial or physical capital would be a "pure" income elasticity; the income coefficient which resulted from human capital would include the non-market efficiency effect and would tend to be further from unity.

Appendix C

THE PURPOSE OF this appendix is to report on some of the modifications in the analysis of the 1960 BLS data discussed in Chapter 4. These cover (1) disaggregating the "goods" into two items for a total of three components of expenditures: services, perishables, and nonperishable goods; (2) dealing with zero expenditures for various market goods; (3) including a race variable in the Engel curves; (4) replacing the education variable with three education dummies; (5) using total current consumption expenditures as the income variable; and (6) considering the relationship between the estimated income elasticities and education coefficients.

1. PERISHABLES-NONPERISHABLES

The Engel curve was fitted to total expenditures for perishables (tobacco, food at home, and alcohol) and for nonperishables (housing, housefurnishings and equipment, clothing, reading and automobiles) with the double-log equation discussed in Chapter 4. The results are shown below (with t values in parentheses):

Item	ln Consumption	ln Education	Age	Family Size	Region	$\bar{R}^2$
Perishables	0.711 (20.44)	−0.237 (−5.69)	−0.002 (−1.33)	0.101 (4.13)	−0.136 (−8.00)	.97
Nonperishables	1.03 (49.68)	0.011 (0.45)	−0.004 (−4.15)	−0.004 (−0.27)	−0.011 (−1.06)	.99

Evidently, when perishable goods, nonperishable goods, and services are considered as three separate items, the luxury item (services) has a positive education effect, the necessity item (perishables) has a negative education effect, while the third item's income elasticity is not significantly different from unity (a t value of 1.45) and its education elasticity is not statistically different from zero. Thus, this grouping of total expenditures is qualitatively consistent with the neutrality model of Chapter 2. Notice that the income elasticity of this more homogeneous goods item is approximately unity, and that neither family size nor the region dummy effect is significant. Notice, too, that age is again observed to affect the durables category.

2. ZERO VALUES

The problem caused by an observation containing zero expenditure for an item is a perplexing one. A zero expenditure for an observation is an extreme value in any of the scatter diagrams. Clearly the fit is improved if the observation is deleted, but in the process some information is lost. On the other hand, allowing a few extreme points to dictate a linear form for the regression seems an excessive adjustment. One alternative is to use some statistical technique other than least squares to estimate a relationship.[1] Another procedure is to replace the zeros by a small value, which is the procedure followed in this study—the zero expenditure per year is replaced in Chapter 4 by an expenditure of one dollar per year. The frequency with which the zero values occur for the dozen or so items discussed in Chapter 4 ranges from eleven observations (7 per cent) to none, as shown in the following table:

Item	Number of Zero Values	Item	Number of Zero Values
Education	11		
Tobacco	6	Automobiles	1
Alcohol	5	Utilities	1
Travel (not auto)	4	Housefurnishings	1
Food (away)	2	Recreation	1
Food (home)	1	All others	0

However, it is clearly arbitrary what value is used to replace the zeros. To determine how sensitive the results were to the value used, regressions were rerun using 0.001 (one tenth of a cent per year). There were no appreciable effects on composite items that did not

---

[1] For example, probit analysis is one alternative. A comparison of results of Engel curve estimates from the 1960 BLS data using probit and least squares is the subject of Mei-chu Wang's dissertation "Problems in the Estimation of Indifference Surfaces Due to Non-Negativity Constraints," University of Rochester, 1967.

have a 0.001 as a final dependent variable.[2] The greatest effects, of course, were on the three items with the most zero values and the smallest average expenditures:

Item	ln *Consumption*	ln *Education*	*Age*	*Family Size*	*Region*	$\bar{R}^2$
Education	1.766	0.542	−0.039	0.529	0.530	.68
	(3.64)	(0.93)	(−1.60)	(1.55)	(2.24)	
Tobacco	0.723	−0.852	−0.034	0.035	−0.044	.70
	(5.32)	(−5.24)	(−5.08)	(0.36)	(−0.66)	
Alcohol	1.666	−0.832	−0.033	−0.248	−0.629	.81
	(9.02)	(−3.76)	(−3.59)	(−1.91)	(−6.97)	

As expected, the use of a more extreme value reduced the $\bar{R}^2$, increased some of the standard errors, and altered some of the coefficients.

The regressions were also run after the observations with zero values were removed. The number of observations for each of these regressions was 157 minus the corresponding number listed in the table above. The regression results using double logs are given in Table C.1 (A). These results more closely resemble those in the text (which set zeros equal to 1.0) than do the results that use zero $\cong 0.001$. Since the zeros are extreme values, the $\bar{R}^2$ is improved by omitting those values, as seen by comparing the $\bar{R}^2$'s in Table C.1 with those in Table 1.

When these items were run linearly, the implied elasticities (analogous to those in Table 3) were as follows:

Mean Elasticities, Zero Values Omitted

Item	*Income*	*Education*	*Family Size*	$\bar{R}^2$
Education (expenditure)	2.721	1.389	−1.102	.695
Tobacco	0.527	−0.576	0.198	.818
Alcohol	1.457	−0.357	−0.401	.837
Food (away)	1.451	−0.012	−0.591	.899
Food (home)	0.526	−0.117	0.548	.950
Housefurnishings	1.031	0.038	0.233	.924

These mean elasticities are again similar to those shown in the text which include the zero values (as zeros). Table C.1 (B) gives the

---

[2] For example, a household which spent zero for utilities and $500.00 for shelter had as the dependent variable 501.00 versus 500.001, with no appreciable effect on the coefficients. This was also true for the goods-services dichotomy.

TABLE C.1
Regression Equations With Zero Values Removed

(A)
Constant Income Elasticity (with ln E)[a]

	ln Consumption	ln Education	Age	Family Size	Region	$\bar{R}^2$
Education	1.557	1.693	0.031	0.520	0.434	.878
	(7.08)	(6.30)	(2.75)	(3.36)	(4.09)	
Tobacco	0.756	−0.803	−0.034	−0.012	−0.009	.870
	(9.45)	(−8.33)	(−8.39)	(−0.21)	(−0.22)	
Alcohol	1.586	−0.463	−0.019	−0.198	−0.550	.910
	(13.78)	(−3.31)	(−3.26)	(−2.44)	(−9.74)	
Food (away)	1.196	0.250	0.004	−0.074	0.072	.941
	(17.49)	(3.05)	(1.18)	(−1.54)	(2.17)	
Food (home)	0.676	−0.213	−0.001	0.108	−0.122	.970
	(21.23)	(−5.58)	(−0.43)	(4.78)	(−7.84)	
Housefurnishings	1.011	−0.092	−0.009	0.139	0.127	.946
	(14.65)[b]	(−1.12)	(−2.67)	(2.84)	(3.78)	

(B)
Constant Income Elasticity (with E)[a]

	ln Consumption	Education	Age	Family Size	Region	$(\bar{\epsilon}_E)$	$\bar{R}^2$
Education	1.579	0.169	0.025	0.495	0.376	(1.705)	.884
	(7.72)	(7.06)	(2.56)	(3.50)	(3.60)		
Tobacco	0.741	−0.080	−0.031	0.005	0.019	(−0.797)	.879
	(10.01)	(−9.24)	(−8.76)	(0.09)	(0.49)		
Alcohol	1.609	−0.052	−0.019	−0.213	−0.530	(−0.518)	.914
	(14.82)	(−4.06)	(−3.66)	(−2.83)	(−9.46)		
Food (away)	1.241	0.017	0.001	−0.111	0.070	(0.174)	.940
	(18.64)	(2.23)	(0.30)	(−2.39)	(2.04)		
Food (home)	0.670	−0.021	0.000	0.113	−0.115	(−0.209)	.970
	(22.20)	(−5.94)	(0.15)	(5.39)	(−7.40)		
Housefurnishings	0.994	−0.006	−0.008	0.153	0.128	(−0.062)	.946
	(14.96)[b]	(−0.80)	(−2.57)	(3.32)	(3.76)		

[a] t values are in parentheses.

[b] Coefficient not statistically different from one (the t values for testing the difference from unity are 0.16 for housefurnishings in (A) and −0.10 in (B)).

results obtained from entering the education variable linearly while excluding the zero value observations.

The results shown here suggest that relatively few important changes occur in the coefficients, their statistical significance, or the coefficient of determination as a consequence of removing the zero values rather than replacing them by a value of 1 (ln (1) = 0) in the log regressions, or leaving them in as zeros in the linear regressions. There are greater differences, however, if the zeros are replaced by some small value such as 0.001.

3. THE EFFECT OF RACE

Another environmental variable which could have an independent effect on consumption is race. Differences in the quality of schooling may appreciably affect the stock of human capital, and if such differences are systematically related to race, the race variable may act as a proxy for school quality and thereby affect expenditure patterns. Further, if different ethnic groups within the economy have significantly different environments, this could also have an effect on behavior. To determine whether race has a discernible independent and systematic effect on expenditure patterns, the percentage of nonwhite households in each cell was included in the Engel curves. This variable was included both as a replacement for the education variable and in addition to it. The results for the goods-services dichotomy are given below (with t values in parentheses).

Item	ln Consumption	ln Education	Per Cent Nonwhite	Age	Family Size	Region	$\bar{R}^2$
Goods	0.884 (59.94)		−0.001 (−0.98)	−0.001 (−2.06)	0.061 (7.48)	−0.045 (−5.71)	.995
Goods	0.920 (57.66)	−0.078 (−4.56)	−0.001 (−1.82)	−0.003 (−4.87)	0.030 (2.90)	−0.040 (−5.25)	.996
Services	1.235 (42.48)		0.001 (0.70)	+0.000 (0.18)	−0.134 (−8.43)	0.105 (6.71)	.986
Services	1.143 (38.18)	0.200 (6.20)	0.002 (1.85)	0.006 (4.80)	−0.056 (−2.90)	0.091 (6.38)	.989

The substitution of the race variable for the education level results in a poorer fit, reduced significance for several of the variables, and a movement away from one in income elasticity.[3] Including the race variable in addition to education, on the other hand, improves the fit slightly and increases the significance of the education, age, and family-size coefficients. The race variable itself is also significant, and suggests that the larger the fraction of nonwhites, ceteris paribus, the larger the share of services in total expenditures.

The results for the thirteen separate items are given in Tables C.2 and C.3. Replacing the education variable with the race variable generally reduces the $\bar{R}^2$ and shifts the income elasticity away from one. Including both education and the nonwhite percentage generally

---

[3] This is as one would expect with the new variable as a poorer proxy for nonmarket efficiency, since the income variable picks up some of the consumption income effect.

TABLE C.2

Expenditure Functions With Race Variable Replacing Education, 1960 BLS Data[a]

Dependent Variable	ln Consumption	Per Cent Nonwhite	Age	Family Size	Region	$\bar{R}^2$
Food (home)	0.5957 (13.05)	0.0032 (1.76)	0.0062 (4.06)	0.1952 (7.80)	−0.1571 (−6.39)	.937
Food (away)	1.3121 (17.26)	−0.0016 (−0.54)	−0.0039 (−1.52)	−0.1775 (−4.26)	0.0951 (2.32)	.924
Tobacco	0.5019 (4.95)	0.0132 (3.28)	−0.0093 (−2.75)	0.2810 (5.05)	−0.1284 (−2.35)	.788
Alcohol	1.5384 (12.47)	0.0153 (3.13)	−0.0069 (−1.68)	−0.0588 (−0.87)	−0.6822 (−10.27)	.895
Shelter	0.8128 (22.06)	−0.0044 (−2.99)	−0.0017 (−1.39)	−0.1251 (−6.19)	−0.1265 (−6.38)	.960
Household operations	1.3158 (31.84)	0.0018 (1.11)	−0.0025 (−1.83)	−0.2329 (−10.27)	0.1866 (8.39)	.971
Housefurnishings and equipment	1.0472 (14.64)	0.0061 (2.14)	−0.0065 (−2.70)	0.1537 (3.92)	0.0830 (2.16)	.939
Clothing	1.2782 (31.44)	0.0046 (2.89)	−0.0048 (−3.50)	0.0595 (2.67)	0.0821 (3.75)	.983
Personal care	0.9379 (25.38)	0.0042 (2.86)	−0.0066 (−5.35)	0.0276 (1.36)	0.1313 (6.60)	.974
Medical care	0.8224 (13.14)	−0.0016 (−0.63)	0.0072 (3.42)	0.0075 (0.22)	0.0427 (1.27)	.888
Leisure	1.3375 (26.44)	−0.0026 (−1.30)	−0.0114 (−6.74)	−0.0766 (−2.76)	−0.0416 (−1.53)	.976
Education	2.4120 (10.10)	−0.0001 (−0.01)	−0.0254 (−3.19)	−0.1348 (−1.03)	0.4939 (3.86)	.851
Travel	1.1607 (14.83)	0.0003 (0.09)	−0.0157 (−6.00)	0.1497 (3.49)	0.0560 (1.33)	.951

[a] *t* values are in parentheses.

TABLE C.3

Expenditure Functions With Race Variable and Education, 1960 BLS Data[a]

Dependent Variable	ln Consumption	ln Education	Per Cent Nonwhite	Age	Family Size	Region	$\bar{R}^2$
Food (home)	0.6695 (13.06)	−0.1607 (−2.91)	0.0023 (1.27)	0.0013 (0.56)	0.1317 (4.02)	−0.1455 (−5.99)	.940
Food (away)	1.2189 (14.11)	0.2027 (2.18)	−0.0005 (−0.15)	0.0024 (0.62)	−0.0974 (−1.77)	0.0805 (1.96)	.926
Tobacco	0.8517 (8.36)	−0.7611 (−6.94)	0.0089 (2.49)	−0.0328 (−7.29)	−0.0197 (−0.30)	−0.0735 (−1.52)	.839
Alcohol	1.7762 (12.97)	−0.5172 (−3.51)	0.0124 (2.59)	−0.0228 (−3.78)	−0.2632 (−3.01)	−0.6449 (−9.93)	.902
Shelter	0.7154 (18.16)	0.2120 (5.00)	−0.0032 (−2.30)	0.0048 (2.77)	−0.0413 (−1.64)	−0.1418 (−7.59)	.966
Household operations	1.1623 (28.76)	0.3339 (7.68)	0.0037 (2.62)	0.0077 (4.34)	−0.1009 (−3.91)	0.1625 (8.48)	.979
Housefurnishings and equipment	1.0599 (12.84)	−0.0275 (−0.31)	0.0059 (2.05)	−0.0073 (−2.01)	0.1429 (2.71)	0.0850 (2.17)	.939
Clothing	1.2778 (27.23)	0.0007 (0.01)	0.0046 (2.84)	−0.0047 (−2.30)	0.0598 (1.99)	0.0820 (3.69)	.983
Personal care	0.9861 (23.52)	−0.1048 (−2.32)	0.0036 (2.45)	−0.0099 (−5.33)	−0.0138 (−0.52)	0.1389 (6.99)	.974
Medical care	0.8122 (11.24)	0.0223 (0.29)	−0.0014 (−0.57)	0.0079 (2.46)	0.0163 (0.35)	0.0411 (1.20)	.887
Leisure	1.2746 (22.18)	0.1368 (2.21)	−0.0018 (−0.91)	−0.0072 (−2.85)	−0.0225 (−0.61)	−0.0515 (−1.89)	.977
Education	1.7082 (6.88)	1.5314 (5.73)	0.0086 (0.99)	0.0217 (1.98)	0.4703 (2.96)	0.3835 (3.26)	.877
Travel	1.3574 (16.10)	−0.4279 (−4.72)	−0.0021 (−0.72)	−0.0289 (−7.78)	−0.0193 (−0.36)	0.0869 (2.17)	.957

[a] *t* values are in parentheses.

improves the $\bar{R}^2$, has little effect on the magnitude of the income or education coefficient, but tends to reduce their significance somewhat. There was no appreciable effect upon the relationship between these two elasticities. The education and race effects seem to be in opposite directions for these detailed items—in only one case (household operations) are their signs the same, with both statistically significant; however, the negative correlation is certainly not a strong one and these results are not inconsistent with a hypothesis of no relationship between the two variables. Likewise, there is no apparent relationship between the race variable and the income elasticity (with education held fixed), as seen from the following two-way diagram:

Per Cent Nonwhite	*Income Elasticity*		
	$\eta > 1$	$\eta \simeq 1$	$\eta < 1$
(+)	Alcohol Household operations Clothing	Housefurnishings and equipment Personal care	Tobacco
(0)	Food (away) Leisure Education Travel		Food (home) Medical care
(−)			Housing

From these results, one concludes that there appears to be no systematic relationship between the effect on expenditures of this race variable and either income or education. This tentative conclusion, however, is subject to the qualification in footnote 16 of Chapter 4.

4. EDUCATION DUMMIES

Most of the regressions discussed so far have assumed that the effect of education on productivity and on the derived demand is proportionate at all levels of education—that the education coefficient is a constant elasticity. The procedure of using double logs also implies that small changes in the education level will have a distinguishable and continuous effect. To relax these conditions somewhat the (ln E) variable was replaced by three education dummy variables designed to examine the effect of broader changes in education—from grade school to high school, from high school to college, et cetera—and to see if the relative effects diminish or increase as education rises.

The four education classes were grade school (0 through 8 years), high school (8–12), college (13–16), and postgraduate (17+), and the three dummies were defined to show the *marginal* effects of each category. Thus, E_1 shows the effect of having a high school education relative to having only grade school training, E_2 shows the effect of college relative to high school, and E_3 shows the effect of postgraduate work relative to college. The effect of, say, college relative to grade school would be $(E_1 + E_2)$, and so forth. The results for the goods-services dichotomy are as follows (with t values in parentheses):

	Item	
Explanatory Variable	*Goods*	*Services*
ln Consumption	0.930 (75.54)	1.137 (49.04)
E_1	−0.034 (−3.26)	0.079 (4.05)
E_2	−0.034 (−4.05)	0.080 (5.03)
E_3	−0.007 (−0.47)	0.017 (0.60)
Age	−0.003 (−4.53)	0.005 (3.91)
Family size	0.026 (2.99)	−0.058 (−3.48)
Region	−0.040 (−5.76)	0.089 (6.85)
$\bar{R}^2$	.996	.989

The effect of this substitution of three dummies for ln E is seen by comparing these equations with those in Chapter 4. There is no important change in the magnitude, sign, or significance of the coefficients of the four other variables. For the education effect itself, the regressions suggest that the magnitude of the effect is quite similar for high school relative to grade school and college relative to high school, while the effect of additional education is small. Similarly, the significance of the first two dummies is roughly the same. In neither case is the postgraduate dummy significant. In all cases the sign is consistent with the neutrality model.

The same regression was run for the thirteen detailed expenditure items. These results are given in Table C.4. Again, the use of the dummies seems to have had little effect on the other variables' coefficients—no significant coefficient changed in sign. The $\bar{R}^2$ is generally increased by the use of the dummies despite the introduction of two additional independent variables; leisure and housefurnishings are the only exceptions.

TABLE C.4
Expenditure Functions With Education Dummy Variables[a]

Dependent Variable	ln Consumption	E_1	E_2	E_3	Age	Family Size	Region	$\bar{R}^2$
Household operations	1.1339 (38.38)	0.1178 (4.76)	0.1450 (7.16)	0.0837 (2.27)	0.0054 (3.20)	−0.0983 (−4.62)	0.1587 (9.56)	.982
Clothing	1.2334 (34.22)	0.0389 (1.29)	−0.0398 (−1.61)	−0.1272 (−2.83)	−0.0029 (−1.39)	0.0774 (2.98)	0.1181 (5.83)	.983
Personal care	0.9480 (30.42)	−0.0242 (−0.93)	−0.0731 (−3.42)	−0.1325 (−3.41)	−0.0084 (−4.72)	−0.0011 (−0.05)	0.1752 (9.99)	.977
Medical care	0.8242 (14.85)	−0.0458 (−0.99)	0.1007 (2.65)	−0.1219 (−1.76)	0.0055 (1.74)	0.0056 (0.14)	0.0255 (0.82)	.892
Leisure	1.3356 (29.29)	0.0794 (2.08)	0.0104 (0.33)	0.0345 (0.61)	−0.0075 (−2.86)	−0.0484 (−1.47)	−0.0641 (−2.50)	.976
Education	1.7749 (9.36)	0.3349 (2.11)	0.7381 (5.68)	0.2502 (1.06)	0.0001 (0.01)	0.3507 (2.57)	0.3278 (3.08)	.884
Travel	1.3561 (21.18)	−0.2544 (−4.75)	−0.1432 (−3.26)	−0.0502 (−0.63)	−0.0304 (−8.32)	−0.0306 (−0.66)	0.1016 (2.86)	.960
Food (home)	0.6197 (15.36)	−0.0677 (−2.01)	−0.0629 (−2.27)	−0.0556 (−1.10)	0.0023 (1.00)	0.1522 (5.25)	−0.1217 (−5.37)	.940
Food (away)	1.2914 (19.27)	0.1670 (2.98)	−0.0089 (−0.19)	−0.0833 (−1.00)	0.0043 (1.13)	−0.1227 (−2.55)	0.0819 (2.17)	.928
Tobacco	0.6236 (7.94)	−0.2957 (−4.50)	−0.2330 (−4.33)	−0.4217 (−4.31)	−0.0263 (−5.86)	0.0877 (1.55)	0.8238 (0.54)	.845
Alcohol	1.5445 (14.28)	−0.1628 (−1.80)	−0.2259 (−3.05)	−0.2867 (−2.13)	−0.0165 (−2.67)	−0.1604 (−2.06)	−0.5352 (−8.80)	.902
Housefurnishings and equipment	0.9715 (14.79)	−0.0676 (−1.23)	0.0243 (0.54)	−0.0658 (−0.80)	−0.0091 (−2.44)	0.1641 (3.47)	0.1187 (3.21)	.938
Shelter	0.7916 (24.81)	0.0565 (3.11)	0.0740 (3.44)	0.0563 (1.43)	0.0033 (0.12)	−0.0915 (−4.38)	−0.1722 (−9.69)	.964

[a] t values are in parentheses.

Turning to a qualitative comparison of the three education co-efficients in relation to the income elasticity and the neutrality model, the findings for the thirteen regressions are summarized as follows:

Education Class	Number of Items Qualitatively Consistent With the Neutrality Model
High school dummy (E_1)	10
College dummy (E_2)	6
Postgraduate dummy (E_3)	8
College-grade school ($E_1 + E_2$)	8
Postgraduate-grade school ($E_1 + E_2 + E_3$)	9

The effects of education vis-à-vis the neutrality model appear to be stronger at lower levels of education, but there does not appear to be any systematic change in the magnitude of the education effect from one schooling dummy to another. Comparing these regressions with those in the text, the improvement in the $\bar{R}^2$, which is slight in most cases (with the exception of tobacco), must be weighed against the convenience of the double-log form, from which the constant education elasticities allow us to estimate the elasticity of consumption income.

5. TOTAL CURRENT CONSUMPTION EXPENDITURE

As was mentioned briefly in Chapter 4 in connection with the goods-services dichotomy, the total consumption expenditure item includes both durable goods and the somewhat unsatisfactory shelter expenditure (which includes rent paid but excludes both mortgage principal repayment and a return on owner's equity). The shelter variable was redefined in terms of rental payments and the independent variable C was replaced by C^*, defined as (C — housefurnishings — automobile expenditures — shelter + rental variable). The simple correlation matrix of the independent variables in the two cases is given in Table C.5 below ((A) contains 157 observations and (B) only 148, since the rental variable is not defined for cells with no renters).

Table C.6 shows the results of substituting C^* for C in regressions on the same set of dependent variables. Since C^* includes the rental item as defined in the text, the percentage of households in the cell which rent their homes was also added as an explanatory variable. In only two cases did that variable have a t value greater than 2.0, and those two are reported here:

Item	ln C^*	ln Education	Age	Family Size	Region	Per Cent Renters	$\bar{R}^2$
Medical care	0.829 (12.03)	−0.091 (−1.10)	−0.004 (−1.07)	−0.006 (−1.18)	0.035 (1.08)	−0.496 (−3.25)	.896
Utilities	0.409 (6.69)	0.011 (0.14)	0.002 (0.46)	0.009 (1.99)	−0.133 (−4.70)	−0.555 (−4.10)	.868

A comparison of Table C.6 with Table 1 again reveals no statistically significant coefficients changing signs. Most of the $\bar{R}^2$'s are higher in Table C.6 (notably tobacco), while the $\bar{R}^2$'s of the durable items are lower; only the housing regression seems appreciably affected by the use of this new consumption variable, undoubtedly due to the different definitions of the housing variable.

TABLE C.5

Simple Correlation Matrix

(A)

Total Consumption Expenditure

	ln Education	Region	ln Consumption	Family Size
Age	−0.730	0.035	−0.698	−0.633
ln Education		−0.234	0.588	0.228
Region			−0.227	0.074
ln Consumption				0.815

(B)

Total Current Consumption Expenditure

	ln Education	Region	ln C^*	Family Size	Per Cent Renters
Age	−0.733	0.035	−0.671	−0:638	0.153
ln Education		−0.235	0.596	0.232	−0.099
Region			−0.270	0.072	−0.023
ln C^*				0.790	−0.619
Family size					−0.667

The regressions were also run with the $(\ln C^*) \cdot (\ln E)$ and $(\ln C^*) \cdot (A)$ interaction effects, both with and without the percentage of renters as an additional variable. Table C.7 indicates the implied elasticities for each item from the "best fit" of the four regression forms. Of the constant elasticity estimates in Table C.6, nine of the fourteen education coefficients are consistent with the neutrality

TABLE C.6
Total Current Consumption Expenditure[a]

Dependent Variable	ln C*	ln Education	Age	Family Size[b]	Region	R̄²
Food (home)	0.6884 (14.05)	−0.2114 (−3.71)	−0.0021 (−0.88)	0.0145 (4.51)	−0.1120 (−4.90)	.9430
Food (away)	1.2468 (15.05)	0.1857 (1.93)	−0.0032 (−0.80)	−0.0059 (−1.09)	0.1026 (2.66)	.9287
Tobacco	0.8225 (8.55)	−0.8600 (−7.70)	−0.0370 (−7.92)	0.0002 (0.03)	0.0115 (0.26)	.8493
Alcohol	1.7623 (13.42)	−0.6880 (−4.51)	−0.0320 (−5.01)	−0.0223 (−2.59)	−0.5150 (−8.41)	.9069
Housing	0.8735 (19.17)	0.1522 (2.88)	0.0010 (0.44)	−0.0137 (−4.60)	−0.1738 (−8.18)	.9505
Household operations	1.1591 (31.99)	0.2739 (6.51)	0.0023 (1.29)	−0.0061 (−2.56)	0.2108 (12.47)	.9822
Housefurnishings and equipment	0.9820 (11.44)[c]	−0.0696 (−0.70)	−0.0121 (−2.89)	0.0209 (3.71)	0.1337 (3.34)	.9317
Clothing	1.2703 (27.62)	−0.0805 (−1.51)	−0.0116 (−5.21)	0.0098 (3.25)	0.1383 (6.45)	.9826
Personal care	0.9748 (22.68)[c]	−0.1661 (−3.33)	−0.0153 (−7.29)	0.0018 (0.65)	0.1791 (8.93)	.9722
Medical care	0.8674 (12.37)[c]	−0.0042 (−0.05)	0.0038 (1.11)	0.0027 (0.58)	0.0498 (1.52)	.8887
Leisure	1.3444 (22.16)	0.1023 (1.45)	−0.0135 (−4.57)	0.0002 (0.06)	−0.0309 (−1.09)	.9733
Education	1.5926 (6.44)	1.4814 (5.16)	0.0146 (1.22)	0.0574 (3.54)	0.4580 (3.97)	.8731
Travel	1.3680 (14.62)	−0.4428 (−4.08)	−0.0361 (−7.92)	0.0036 (0.59)	0.0843 (1.93)	.9451
Utilities	0.4519 (7.12)	0.1082 (1.47)	0.0109 (3.53)	0.0190 (4.58)	−0.1163 (−3.93)	.8534

[a] t values are in parentheses.

[b] Family size is in units different by a factor of 10 from previous results.

[c] Not statistically different from one (the t values for testing the difference from unity are −0.21 for housefurnishings, −0.59 for personal care, and − 1.89 for medical care.)

model; in Table C.7, ten are consistent. In comparing the best fit here with those in Table 4 (where comparisons are permissible), we find the major differences in those items which include the percentage of renters as an independent variable (notably medical care, personal care, housefurnishings, and housing), or in those items in which the linear form was the best fit in the text (i.e., tobacco). With all these differences taken into account, the use of C* in place of C still does not appreciably change the overall expenditure patterns discussed in Chapter 4.

TABLE C.7
Expenditure Functions With Income Defined as Total Current
Consumption Expenditures
Form With Highest $\bar{R}^2$

Item	Regression[a] Form	η^*	ϵ_E	ϵ_F	$\bar{R}^2$
Food (home)	4.	0.6908	−0.1613	+0.5975	.9437
Food (away)	4.	1.2265	0.1822	−0.2249	.9312
Tobacco	3.	0.6846	−0.7290	+0.1381	.8548
Alcohol	2.	1.8010	−0.6007	−0.4337	.9081
Housing	2.	0.8833	0.1743	−0.3695	.9507
Utilities	4.	0.3299	0.0620	+0.3084	.8700
Household operations	3.	1.1626	0.2546	−0.2442	.9833
Housefurnishings	2.	0.9565	−0.1272	+0.4851	.9326
Clothing	4.	1.1399	0.0084	+0.3566	.9855
Personal care	4.	0.7932	−0.0376	+0.1253	.9841
Medical care	4.	0.7896	−0.0884	−0.2474	.8963
Leisure	3.	1.3388	0.0897	−0.0321	.9731
Education	1.	1.5926	1.4814	+1.8440	.8731
Travel	4.	1.0933	−0.2918	+0.1028	.9570
Goods	4.	0.9376	−0.1096	+0.1285	.9941
Services	2.	1.1572	0.1275	−0.1381	.9887

[a] Regression forms were: (1) constant elasticity; (2) constant elasticity with the per cent renters as an additional explanatory variable; (3) interaction form discussed in the text; and (4) interaction form with the per cent renters as an additional explanatory variable.

6. THE ELASTICITY OF CONSUMPTION INCOME

Chapters 4, 5, and 6 present several estimates of the relationship between the income and education elasticities. In this section several additional, comparable estimates are shown for other combinations of the Engel curves, all taken from the data in Chapter 4. The purpose here is to present further evidence on the degree of sensitivity in the estimates presented in the text.

Each Engel curve estimates the income elasticity η_i and the education elasticity ϵ_{iE} for a particular market good. The regression discussed in this section take these pairs of elasticities, (η_i, ϵ_{iE}), as observations and regress ϵ_{iE} on η_i. The regression coefficient, b, obtained from fitting

$$\epsilon_{iE} = a + b\eta_i + u_i, \tag{C.1}$$

or

$$\epsilon_{iE} = b(\eta_i - 1) + u_i, \tag{C.2}$$

is an estimate of the elasticity of consumption income ϵ_{Y_cE} as defined in Chapter 2, since equation (2.11) states that

$$\epsilon_{iE} = \epsilon_{Y_eE}(\eta_i - 1).$$

Equations (C.1) and (C.2) differ only when the relevant means of the variables ϵ_{iE} and $(\eta_i - 1)$ and not zero.[4] Although for most of the sets of observations the means are not far from zero, all sets were run both weighted and unweighted for both equations (C.1) and (C.2).

Four additional sets of regressions across the Engel curves are discussed below. These will be denoted by the letters A, B, C, and D here to simplify the exposition. Set "A" includes fifteen constant elasticity Engel curves. The values of ϵ_{iE} and η_i are those given in Table 1 for the following items: food at home, food away, alcohol, housing, household operations, housefurnishings, clothing, personal care, leisure, education, and utilities. For the items tobacco and medical care, the estimates are slightly changed, the differences resulting from omitting the explanatory variables with t values of less than one; for the travel item, the expenditures were broken down into expenditures on automobiles and expenditures on other travel. The two elasticities, η_i and ϵ_{iE}, for these four items are, respectively, 0.758 and -0.819 for tobacco; 0.844 and 0.017 for medical care; 1.378 and -0.526 for automobiles; and 1.605 and -0.110 for travel other than by auto.

Set "B" for the same fifteen items replaces the constant elasticity form with the interaction form for six of the fifteen; the remaining eight are the same observations as in "A." The interaction effects for housing, automobiles, and other travel are given in the table of "best fits" (Table 4) in the text. For the remaining three—food at home, housefurnishings, and utilities—the interaction mean elasticities ($\bar{\eta}_i$ and $\bar{\epsilon}_{iE}$) are, respectively, 0.614 and -0.145, 0.961 and -0.045, and 0.430 and 0.130.

---

[4] Weighting by expenditures and summing over all goods, equation (C.1) becomes

$$\sum_i X_i \epsilon_{iE} = a \sum_i X_i + b \sum_i \eta_i X_i + \sum_i u_i X_i.$$

Dividing by the sum of the expenditures,

$$\bar{\epsilon}_E = a + b\bar{\eta} + \bar{u}$$

where the bar denotes a weighted mean. Since $\epsilon_E = 0$, $\bar{\eta} = 1$, and $\bar{u} = 0$, $-a = b$. So the weighted regression is also run as

$$\epsilon_{iE} = b(\eta_i - 1) + u_i.$$

Verbally, when weighted, the point of means of ϵ_{iE} and $(\eta_i - 1)$ is the origin.

TABLE C.8

Relationship Between Income and Education Elasticities Across Items[a]

Set	Means				Simple Correlation $(\epsilon_{iE}\eta_i)$		Regression[b]					
	Weighted		Unweighted				$\epsilon_{iE} = a + b\eta_i + u_i$ Weighted		$\epsilon_{iE} = a + b\eta_i + u_i$ Unweighted		$\epsilon_{iE} = b(\eta_i - 1) + u_i$ Weighted	
	ϵ_{iE}	η_i	ϵ_{iE}	η_i	Weighted	Unweighted	a	b	a	b	b	
A	−0.03	1.02	+0.02	1.11	−0.052	+0.210	0.070 (0.26)	−0.161 (−0.60)	−0.326 (−0.70)	0.309 (0.77)	−0.117 (−0.44)	
B	+0.01	0.97	+0.05	1.07	+0.142	+0.310	−0.107 (−0.44)	0.086 (0.33)	−0.456 (−1.01)	0.474 (1.18)	0.112 (0.42)	
C	+0.01	0.96	+0.05	1.07	+0.155	+0.326	−0.081 (−0.39)	0.070 (0.31)	−0.478 (−1.08)	0.492 (1.25)	0.083 (0.42)	
D	−0.02	0.92	+0.05	1.11	+0.522	+0.473	−0.571 (−3.59)	0.629 (3.10)	−0.929 (−1.29)	0.881 (1.42)	0.496 (3.75)	

[a] See pp. 127, 129 for definition of sets A–D.
[b] t values are in parentheses.

Set "C" is the same as the fifteen items given in Table 4, except for the substitution of the tobacco and medical care observations from set "A" described above. Set "D" is a subset of set "A," containing only the nine nondurable items: food at home, food away, tobacco, alcohol, household operations, personal care, medical care, leisure, and education. This nondurables set was considered most likely to be free of the durables bias discussed in Appendix B.

Table C.8 summarizes the regressions—weighted and unweighted—for these four sets of items. This evidence suggests again that the positive consumption income effect is considerably higher in the unweighted case, and much higher when estimated from only the nondurable items. Naturally, the results shown in the text most closely resemble those in set "C." If, in fact, the durables bias discussed in Appendix B is an important factor in these Engel curves, then the findings for set "D" may be the least biased, and this would suggest that the elasticity of real income with respect to education is somewhat larger than the value presented in Chapter 4. This finding for nondurables is qualitatively consistent with the conclusion reached at the end of Chapter 5; quantitatively the two sets of nondurables are not entirely comparable, and hence the magnitudes of the estimated coefficients differ.

Appendix D

1. AN ADDITIONAL CROSS-CLASSIFICATION: BY OCCUPATION

AS MENTIONED IN Chapter 6, the 1950 BLS expenditure survey is available in published form with an additional cross-classification by occupation (seven groups). Of the 756 cells in this four-way cross-tabulation of the North region, 251 (or one-third of the cells) were empty, leaving 505 observations. Of these, 111 (or more than one-fifth) contained only one household, and only fifty-nine (or one-tenth) of the cells contained thirty or more households. Thus, investigating the relationship between expenditures, income, and education across these 505 cells is an approximation to dealing with the individual households themselves, and can be expected to incorporate both the advantages and disadvantages of individual data.

The two principal disadvantages of these smaller cells (or of individual data) are the problems of zero expenditures on items and the problems of biases due to measurement error. The number of zero values for expenditures is greater in these 505 observations—for example, 152 cells spent zero on educational expenditures (i.e., 30 per cent of the cells compared to 7 per cent in the 1960 data used), and three cells spent zero on as common an item as food at home! In the light of the second section of Appendix C, these zeros were replaced with a value of 1.0 in the log regressions $(\ln(1) = 0)$. As discussed in Appendix B and in several references cited there, the main advantage of using grouped data is that, when they are appropriately cross-classified, a better proxy for permanent income can be obtained. But this advantage is clearly dissipated as the cells become smaller and smaller in size. Since the average cell in these 505 observations contains approximately eleven households, the proxy for permanent income and expenditure on durable items will presumably contain greater measurement error.

The results of the regressions on the 505 observations for the detailed expenditures are given in Table D.1. (The housing variable here is the total shelter expenditure plus utilities, and so it is not comparable to the housing variable discussed in Chapter 6. The travel item here is the sum of the two travel items shown in Table 21.) The results can be compared with Table 21; the two items (other than housing) with the most important changes in income or education effects are travel and medical care. There does not appear to be any systematic shift in the income elasticity toward or away from unity (six items moved toward, six away), or in the education elasticity toward or away from zero (five toward, seven away). Given the constraint on the mean η and the mean ϵ_E, there cannot be any systematic shift upward or downward.

With these results approximately one-half of the items (or 42 per cent of total consumption) as compared with 60 per cent of the items

TABLE D.1

Regression Equations for Consumption Items, 1950 BLS Data, North Region, 505 Observations[a]

Dependent Variable	ln Consumption	ln Education	Age	Family Size	$\bar{R}^2$
Food (home)	0.507	−0.192	−0.001	0.021	.80
	(15.21)	(−4.82)	(−0.64)	(11.30)	
Food (away)	1.458	0.073	−0.010	−0.031	.52
	(15.79)	(0.66)	(−3.00)	(−6.12)	
Tobacco	0.762	−0.841	−0.033	0.010	.57
	(9.38)	(−8.67)	(−11.27)	(2.29)	
Alcohol	1.536	−1.323	−0.034	−0.008	.51
	(12.11)	(−8.74)	(−7.63)	(−1.18)	
Housing	0.758	0.240	0.009	−0.009	.75
	(25.11)	(6.67)	(7.88)	(−5.21)	
Household operations	1.352	0.460	0.013	−0.019	.85
	(34.29)	(9.77)	(9.27)	(−8.51)	
Housefurnishings	1.369	−0.450	−0.024	0.001	.74
	(18.64)	(−5.24)	(−9.02)	(0.24)	
Clothing	1.320	−0.138	−0.011	0.003	.92
	(39.01)	(−3.41)	(−8.98)	(1.62)	
Personal care	0.903	−0.108	−0.009	0.003	.89
	(31.12)	(−3.11)	(−8.26)	(1.73)	
Medical care	0.826	−0.002	0.001	0.006	.62
	(14.47)	(−0.03)	(0.29)	(1.90)	
Leisure	1.294	−0.154	−0.011	0.006	.89
	(31.09)	(−3.09)	(−7.74)	(2.38)	
Education	1.716	0.794	−0.001	0.014	.50
	(10.08)	(3.91)	(−0.19)	(1.48)	
Travel	1.500	−0.159	−0.010	−0.002	.74
	(20.81)	(−1.85)	(−3.76)	(−0.58)	

[a] t values are in parentheses.

(or 65 per cent of total consumption) are consistent with the neutrality model for education. The resulting implied elasticity of consumption income, measured as an average of $\epsilon_{iE}/(\eta_i - 1)$ over the items, and excluding the biased housing variable, is 0.219 unweighted or 0.019 weighted. These results are significantly weaker than those reported in Chapter 6. For the reasons discussed at the beginning of this appendix, it is felt that the results in Chapter 6 give a more accurate picture of the shifts in expenditure patterns as income or education changes.

2. THE GAINFULLY EMPLOYED

Of the 505 observations from the 1950 BLS data discussed in the previous section, sixty-nine concerned a group of families whose occupation was reported as "not gainfully employed." Since these sixty-nine differed significantly from the other 436 observations in several characteristics, they were omitted in the regressions discussed in this section.

For a comparison of the means of several characteristics of the two subsamples, see Table D.2. The results of the weighted regressions for goods and services are as follows (with t values in parentheses):

TABLE D.2

Selected Means and Coefficients of Variation for Subsamples of the 1950 BLS Data, North Region[a]

Variable	All Households	Gainfully Employed	Not Gainfully Employed
Family size			
Mean	3.0	3.1	2.4
Coefficient of variation	28	25	41
Age			
Mean	47	44	64
Coefficient of variation	20	15	10
ln Education			
Mean (antilog)	2.27 (9.7 years)	2.29 (9.9 years)	2.12 (8.4 years)
Coefficient of variation	13	13	13
ln Consumption			
Mean (antilog)	5.87 ($3,560)	5.94 ($3,810)	5.40 ($2,220)
Coefficient of variation	8	7	11

[a] Sample size is 505 observations for "all households," of which 436 were "gainfully employed" and 69 "not gainfully employed."

Item	ln Consumption	ln Education	Age	Family Size	$\overline{R}^2$
Goods	0.940 (90.58)	−0.082 (−6.49)	−0.002 (−4.64)	0.004 (6.54)	.983
Services	1.161 (40.53)	0.231 (6.59)	0.004 (2.85)	−0.009 (−6.11)	.904

The corresponding regressions for the thirteen items are given in Table D.3. Here, too, only 50 per cent of the items (or 42 per cent of total consumption) are consistent with the neutrality model. But although the unweighted average of ϵ_{Y_cE} of the eleven[1] relevant items is 0.206 and similar to the estimate above, the weighted average here is 0.098 and as such much more similar to the result in the text.

TABLE D.3

Regression Equations for Consumption Items, 1950 BLS Data, North Region,[a] (gainfully employed, 436 observations)

Dependent Variable	ln Consumption	ln Education	Age	Family Size	$\overline{R}^2$
Food (home)	0.5552 (16.00)	−0.2321 (−5.46)	−0.0033 (−2.00)	0.0190 (10.34)	.793
Food (away)	1.3384 (13.40)	0.2709 (2.13)	−0.0015 (−0.31)	−0.0314 (−5.72)	.431
Tobacco	0.7173 (7.90)	−0.7412 (−6.66)	−0.0293 (−6.73)	0.0066 (1.37)	.378
Alcohol	1.5854 (11.30)	−1.2466 (−7.25)	−0.0357 (−5.30)	−0.0133 (−1.79)	.393
Housing	0.7835 (22.81)	0.2007 (4.77)	0.0061 (3.68)	−0.0090 (−4.97)	.734
Household operations	1.3332 (30.71)	0.4882 (9.18)	0.0145 (6.94)	−0.0183 (−7.99)	.835
Housefurnishings	1.4797 (18.65)	−0.5166 (−5.31)	−0.0279 (−7.33)	−0.0054 (−1.30)	.676
Clothing	1.2284 (35.26)	−0.0630 (−1.48)	−0.0053 (−3.17)	0.0038 (2.05)	.899
Personal care	0.8414 (27.61)	−0.0634 (−1.70)	−0.0060 (−4.10)	0.0035 (2.18)	.850
Medical care	0.9525 (15.53)[b]	−0.0960 (−1.28)	−0.0047 (−1.58)	0.0014 (0.44)	.618
Leisure	1.3423 (29.31)	−0.2070 (−3.69)	−0.0163 (−7.41)	0.0034 (1.42)	.860
Education	1.8696 (9.94)	0.8447 (3.67)	0.0056 (0.62)	0.0137 (1.38)	.480
Travel	1.6103 (21.13)	−0.2615 (−2.80)	−0.0172 (−4.70)	−0.0036 (−0.89)	.734

[a] t values are in parentheses.

[b] Coefficient not statistically different from one (the t value for testing the difference from unity is −0.77).

[1] These two averages exclude the biased housing variable as well as the medical care item, since the income elasticity of the latter is not statistically different from unity.

Appendix E

EDUCATIONAL ATTAINMENT IN ISRAEL

THE PURPOSE OF this appendix is to establish the ranking of educational attainment among the four groups in the population of Israel: Euro-American newcomers (EN), Euro-American veterans (EV), Afro-Asian newcomers (AN), and Afro-Asian veterans (AV). (This rankings is used in the second part of Chapter 6.) The relevant findings on this educational attainment, shown by per cent distribution for the year 1954 in the 1959–60 *Statistical Abstract of Israel*, are presented in Table E.1. The levels of schooling were estimated on the basis of the following estimated values:

	Range	Value Used
No school	0 years	0 years
Did not complete primary education	1– 7 years	4 years
Completed primary education	8–11 years	9 years
Completed postprimary education	12–14 years	13 years
Completed higher education	15+ years	16 years

The resulting estimated levels of schooling attained were:

	Newcomers		Veterans		
	Euro-Americans	Afro-Asians	Euro-Americans	Afro-Asians	Israeli
Males	8.2	4.9	10.1	5.5	8.7
Females	7.7	2.6	9.4	3.2	8.3

Note that the ranking is the same for both sexes, and stands as follows (from highest attainment): EV, EN, AV, AN.

TABLE E.1

Educational Attainment of the Jewish Population,
Age Fifteen and Over, in 1954
(per cent distribution)

Educational Level	*EN*	*AN*	*EV*[a]	*AV*	*Israeli*
Males					
Did not attend school	2.6	22.5	1.0	21.8	2.0
Did not complete primary education	33.1	49.5	17.7	39.8	24.0
Completed primary education	41.2	19.5	37.7	28.7	49.8
Completed postprimary education	18.3	7.8	33.4	7.6	21.4
Completed higher education	4.8	0.7	10.2	2.1	2.8
Females					
Did not attend school	6.3	57.8	4.8	53.2	7.3
Did not complete primary education	31.9	26.2	16.3	23.4	21.2
Completed primary education	40.6	13.0	40.4	18.5	48.7
Completed postprimary education	19.2	2.8	33.4	4.5	20.6
Completed higher education	2.0	0.2	5.1	0.4	2.2

Source: *Statistical Abstract of Israel 1959/1960*, pp. 394–95.
[a] Veteran: one who migrated to Israel prior to 1947.

Bibliography

Becker, Gary S. "A Theory of the Allocation of Time." *Economic Journal*, September 1965.

————. "The Allocation of Time and Goods Over Time." New York: NBER, June 1967. (Mimeographed.)

———— and Michael, Robert T. "On the Theory of Consumer Demand." New York: NBER, 1970. (Mimeographed.)

Ben Porath, Yoram. "The Production of Human Capital and the Life Cycle of Earnings." *Journal of Political Economy*, August 1967.

Cramer, J. S. "Efficient Grouping, Regression, and Correlation in Engel Curve Analysis." *Journal of the American Statistical Association*, March 1964.

Friedman, Milton. *A Theory of the Consumption Function*. Princeton: Princeton University Press for NBER, 1957.

Ghez, Gilbert R. "A Theory of Life Cycle Consumption." Ph.D. dissertation, Columbia University, 1970.

Grossman, Michael. "The Demand for Health: A Theoretical and Empirical Investigation." NBER, forthcoming.

Haitovsky, Yoel. "On the Correlation Between Estimated Parameters in Linear Regressions." New York: NBER, May 1969. (Mimeographed.)

————. "Unbiased Multiple Regression Coefficients Estimated From One-Way Classification Tables When the Cross-Classifications Are Unknown." *Journal of the American Statistical Association*, September 1966.

Houthakker, H. S. "An International Comparison of Household Expenditure Patterns, Commemorating the Centenary of Engel's Law." *Econometrica*, October 1957.

Klinov-Malul, Ruth. *The Profitability of Investment in Education in Israel*. Jerusalem: Falk Project for Economic Research in Israel, 1966.

Kosters, Marvin and Welch, Finis. "The Effect of Minimum Wages on the Distribution of Changes in Aggregate Employment." *American Economic Review*, forthcoming.

Lamale, Helen H. and Stotz, Margaret S. "The Interim City Worker's Family Budget." *Monthly Labor Review*, August 1960.

Lancaster, Kelvin J. "Changes and Innovation in the Technology of Consumption." *American Economic Review*, May 1966.

————. "A New Approach to Consumer Demand." *Journal of Political Economy,* April 1966.

Liviatan, Nissan. *Consumption Patterns in Israel.* Jerusalem: Falk Project for Economic Research in Israel, 1964.

————. "Errors in Variables and Engel Curve Analysis." *Econometrica,* July 1961.

Malinvaud, E. *Statistical Methods of Econometrics.* Chicago: Rand McNally and Co., 1966.

Mincer, Jacob. "Market Prices, Opportunity Costs and Income Effects." In *Measurement in Economics: Studies in Mathematical Economics and Econometrics in Memory of Yehuda Grunfeld.* Palo Alto: Stanford University Press, 1963.

Muth, Richard F. "Household Production and Consumer Demand Functions." *Econometrica,* July 1966.

Paroush, Jacob. "Hefreshay Tzrechan Bain Schechavoth Ha-ochlusiah" ["Differences in Consumption Between Various Strata of the Population"]. *Riv'on Le Chalchlah [Economic Quarterly],* June 1966.

Prais, S. J. "A Comment" [on R. Summers's "A Note on Least-Squares Bias in Household Expenditure Analysis"]. *Econometrica,* January 1959.

———— and Houthakker, H. S. *The Analysis of Family Budgets.* Cambridge: Cambridge University Press, 1955.

Reid, Margaret. *Housing and Income.* Chicago: University of Chicago Press, 1962.

Schultz, Theodore W. "Reflections on Investment in Man." *Journal of Political Economy,* October 1962, supplement.

Statistical Abstract of Israel, 1959/1960, No. 11. Jerusalem: The Government Printer.

Theil, H. *Economic Forecasts and Policy.* Amsterdam: North-Holland Press Publishing Company, 1961.

U.S. Government, Department of Labor, Bureau of Labor Statistics. *Study of Consumer Expenditures, Incomes and Savings, 1950,* vols. 1–10. Philadelphia: Wharton School of Finance and Commerce, 1956.

————. *Survey of Consumer Expenditures 1960–61.* BLS Report 237, 1966.

————. *City Worker's Family Budget: Autumn 1966.* BLS Bulletin 1570–1, 1967.

Welch, Finis. "Education in Production." *Journal of Political Economy,* January 1970.

Wang, Mei-chu. "Problems in the Estimation of Indifference Surfaces Due to Non-Negativity Constraints." Ph.D. dissertation, University of Rochester, 1967.

Zellner, Arnold. "An Efficient Method of Estimating Seemingly Unrelated Regressions and Tests for Aggregation Bias." *Journal of the American Statistical Association,* June 1962.

Index